AN ESSAY

ON THE
SCRIPTURAL DOCTRINE
OF
IMMORTALITY

BY THE REV.

JAMES CHALLIS, M.A., F.R.S., F.R.A.S.

PLUMIAN PROFESSOR OF ASTRONOMY AND
EXPERIMENTAL PHILOSOPHY IN THE UNIVERSITY
OF CAMBRIDGE, AND FELLOW OF TRINITY
COLLEGE.

"Anagke gar moi epikeitai ouai gar moi estin, ean me
euaggelzûmai"

—I Cor. ix. 16

I

AN ESSAY
ON THE
SCRIPTURAL DOCTRINE OF IMMORTALITY.

Considering that under the existing conditions of humanity, disease, and decay, and death abound on every side, it is surprising that the word "immortality" obtained a place in systems of philosophy, the authors of which must be supposed to have been unacquainted with divine revelation. It is not surprising that in the absence of such aid the belief of immortality should not have been firmly held, or that by some philosophers it should have been expressly disavowed. Even in the Canonical Scriptures, the words "immortal" and "immortality" occur only in the Epistles of the Apostle Paul, and consequently not till "life and immortality had been brought to light through the Gospel." It is a remarkable circumstance that these words are met with more frequently in the Apocryphal Books, 2 Esdras, Wisdom of Solomon, and Ecclesiasticus, than in the Canonical Scriptures. The explanation of the apparent silence of the Scriptures, especially those of the Old Testament, on so essential a doctrine, will, I think, be found to be given by the course of argument adopted in this essay.

It may, further, be noticed that, according to philosophical dogma not derived from the teaching of Scripture, immortality is regarded as a principle, or innate quality, in virtue of which the human soul is exempt from the experience of death or annihilation. On this account Greek and Roman philosophers speak of "the immortality of *the soul*," and even in the present day the same terms are used, the soul being regarded as *per se* immortal. But neither in the Scriptures, nor in the Apocrypha, is "immortality" qualified by the adjunct "of the soul;" the reason for which may be that since death, as far as our senses inform us, is an *objective* reality, the writers judged that mortality and freedom from mortality could only be predicated of *body*. It must, however, be taken into account that according to the doctrine of Scripture there is "a spiritual body" as well as "a natural body," so that while the natural body is, as we know,

3

subject to the law of death, it may be true that the spiritual body is capable of immortality. This point will be farther discussed in the course of the essay.

To account for the absence of any direct announcement of man's immortality in the Old Testament, and for its being sparingly mentioned in the New Testament, the following argument seems legitimate and sufficient. These Scriptures, as already intimated, give no countenance to the idea that the soul of man possesses any innate principle of immortality; on the contrary, they reveal immortality by revealing *the means* by which the spirit of man is *made* immortal. As, according to natural science, the external world, both the animate part and the inanimate, has become such as we now perceive it to be by processes of generation and development, so there is reason from Scripture to say that a spiritual world is being created in an analogous manner, and that to this creation all other creations are subordinate and contributory. Moreover, we, the subjects of this creation, are so constituted that we are conscious of, and can ourselves take cognizance of, the means by which it is effected. These considerations may be applied to account for the mode in which immortality is treated of in the Bible. It concerns us, above all things, to discern and feel the operations whereby our spirits are formed both intellectually and morally for an immortal existence; and, accordingly, Scripture is full of instruction, addressed both to the understanding and the heart, concerning those means. Thus, although the final effect is not directly named till the scheme of the spiritual creation is completely unfolded, it is yet true that the whole of the Scriptures from beginning to end has relation to man's immortality.

Not only did the philosophy of Greece and Rome fail to substantiate the reality of an immortal existence; other philosophical systems, as well the mystical conceptions of Eastern nations, as the metaphysical speculations of modern Europe, have equally failed to arrive at certainty respecting this verity. Now, it will be found, I think, to be established by the argument of this essay, that in all these instances the cause of failure is the same.

The doctrine cannot, in fact, be understood and believed without an understanding of the means by which the immortal spirit is *formed*, and the ascertainment of those means is beyond the power of unaided human intelligence. Although the evidences of an immortal destiny may be in us and around us, they cannot be discerned apart from enlightenment by a divine revelation as to the purpose and end of the whole creation.

The Scriptures of the Old and New Testaments profess to be a revelation of the mind and will of the Creator of all things. If they are really such, they must be capable of giving the information which, as said above, is necessary for certifying the doctrine of man's immortality. I shall, therefore, with express reference to the title of the essay, first make the *hypothesis* that the Scriptures are indeed a revelation from God, written to reveal His will and His acts, and on this ground I shall proceed to inquire what information can be derived from them respecting the *creation* of the spirit of man for an immortal destiny. The character of the information obtained may possibly suffice to establish both the truth of the hypothesis and the certainty of the doctrine of immortality.

Before commencing the argument, it will be well to state on what principles, and according to what rules, Scripture will be cited for conducting it. It will be supposed that the Holy Scriptures, as a whole, consist of words of God written for our sakes; and although they were written by human authors, under diverse circumstances, and in various ages, the several parts are still to be regarded as having virtually but *one author*, the Holy Spirit, and as constituting on that account a consistent whole. This view is almost necessitated by the noticeable circumstance that very little information is given in the Scriptures themselves respecting the authors of the writings, or the time and place of their composition. This is true, for instance, of such cardinal books as the four Gospels. Respecting these matters enough is said to show that human hands have been employed to write the books of Scripture, while so much has been left unsaid that we must infer that this kind of information is of little moment by reason of the *internal* evidence the Scriptures contain of their divine authorship. Such evidence, it seems to me, is especially given by the fact that the Scriptures present a faithful *transcript* of the world as it has been and is, in respect to the calamities, wars, and revolutions that have befallen nations, and those weaknesses and wickednesses of individuals and peoples, the accounts of which are so great a stumbling-block to the "unstable and the unlearned." These very accounts, it is possible, may be intended to tell us, if rightly inquired into, why these things are so, why there is evil in the world, and what shall be the end of it. The world has existed, it is believed, nearly six thousand years, and at this day we see that many suffer from sorrow and pain, labour and poverty are the lot of a very large proportion of the populations, calamities by fire and water are frequent, plague and pestilence still visit the earth, cruelty and murders are rife, and so far from there being an end of wars, never before have men fabricated such potent implements for killing each other. Such facts as these constitute, after all, the difficulties which beset humanity, and it may be presumed that, with the intent of accounting for their existence, they are put on record in the word of God. On the broad principle that the Author of a world like this will have vouchsafed reasons for its being such as it is, I accept the Scriptures of the Old and New Testaments as the word of God written for this very purpose, and instead of cavilling, as some do, at difficulties which probably have no other foundation than their own ignorance, it will be my endeavour to make use of Scripture for explaining the perplexities and difficulties which actually surround the facts of human experience. The discussion of the particular question I have taken in hand will give occasion for employing the Scriptures in this manner, and in doing so I shall quote from all parts indiscriminately, regarding the whole as sufficiently authoritative and trustworthy for the purposes of the argument.

The above-mentioned general purpose the Scriptures may be supposed to be adequate to fulfil, whether as expressed in the Hebrew tongue, or in that of the Septuagint, or as translated in the English version, notwithstanding that, as must be admitted, faults of transcription, or translation, or interpretation have given rise to many verbal errors. But the difficulties produced by these imperfections are of slight importance in comparison with the great difficulty of discovering how and on what principles to interpret the Scriptures so as to derive from them the particular doctrines they are designed to teach. Amid the great diversity of views that exists relative to modes of interpretation, it may safely be maintained that the foremost and chief requisite for making true deductions from the Scriptures is to have *confidence* in them as being depositions of Divine wisdom. Men of science, in their endeavours to discover the secrets of Nature, are baffled again and again, and yet by little and little they obtain accessions to knowledge just because they never doubt but that Nature, if rightly interrogated, will give them true answers. It seems, therefore, reasonable to expect that the words of God, handled on principles analogous to those which have been successfully applied in acquiring knowledge of His works, might be found capable of answering the hard questions which are now, more, perhaps, than in past times, agitating men's minds. This philosophy, having a surer basis than that of any mere human intellectual system, might be expected to succeed where these have failed. The bearing of these remarks on the main subject of the essay will be seen as we go on.

Commencing now, after the foregoing preliminaries, the general argument, I remark, in the first place, that since, as matter of fact, all men die, they cannot partake of immortality unless they are restored to life after death. We have, therefore, to inquire both as to what the Scriptures say concerning *death*, and what they reveal concerning *resurrection*. Again, it may be taken for granted that as in the natural world, so in the spiritual world, the Creator of all things effects His purposes by operating according to *laws*. On this principle St. Paul in Rom. viii. 2 speaks of "the law of sin and death," meaning that sin and death are invariably related to each other as antecedent and consequent. By an irrevocable law death is ordained to be "the wages of sin" (Rom.

vi. 23). Of ourselves we can judge that it does not consist with the power and wisdom of an omnipotent and omniscient Creator that the sinful should live for ever. But if this be so, it must evidently be true also that immortality, being exemption from death, is the *consequence* of freedom from sin, that is, of perfect righteousness. This is as necessary a law as the other.

Hence the inquiry respecting the means by which man is made immortal resolves itself into inquiring by what means he is made righteous; and, as the first step in this inquiry, we have to consider what Scripture says concerning the entrance of sin and death into the world. If sin be defined to be doing what is contrary to the will of God, as expressed by a command, righteousness, being its opposite, will consist in acting according to His will. Hence sin and righteousness both imply that a revelation of the will of God has been antecedently made, either directly by a command or law, or by the voice of conscience. It is on this principle that St. Paul says, "apart from law sin is dead" (Rom. vii. 8), and in another place speaks of "the righteousness *of the law*" being fulfilled (Rom. viii. 4). Accordingly, when Adam was placed in the garden of Eden, a *command* was expressly given him for trial of his obedience.

The narrative in Scripture of the circumstances under which sin was first committed is deserving of special consideration on account of the instruction it conveys. It states that Eve, knowing that God had commanded Adam not to eat of the tree of the knowledge of good and evil, yet, being deceived by the serpent and enticed by her own desires, "took of the fruit thereof, and did eat, and gave also to her husband with her, and he did eat" (Gen. iii. 6). Thus, as St. Paul writes, "Adam was not deceived, but the woman being deceived was in the transgression" (I Tim. ii. 14). But both partook of the forbidden fruit, and by so doing both sinned alike against their Maker, the deed being sinful, not as considered by itself, but by reason of the antecedent command, which made it an act of *disobedience.*

If we assume that the account of Eve's temptation is to be taken as literally true, so that the tempter had actually the form of

8

a serpent and addressed to her *spoken* words, these facts will have to be regarded as altogether *miraculous*. There are good reasons for admitting this view, when it is considered, first, that the information which this portion of Scripture gives equally concerns all of every age, and in order that it might be intelligible to all, it was necessary that in the infancy of the world it should be conveyed by *objective* representation; and, again, that various instances are met with in the Bible of analogous teaching of essential doctrine by means of miracles. The translation of Enoch, the Deluge, the destruction of Sodom, the plagues of Egypt and deliverance of Israel, the giving of the law from Sinai, the passage of Jordan, the ascension of Elijah, and the resurrection of Christ, are all symbolic miracles, the interpretations of which have intimate relation to the doctrine of man's immortality. This being understood, I shall proceed to discuss particularly the meaning of the Scriptural account of the beginning of sin through temptation by the serpent, and on the supposition that the facts as recorded are real but symbolic, I shall endeavour to deduce from them their doctrinal signification.

The first question to consider is, Why is the tempting spirit called a *serpent*? The Scripture affirms that "the serpent was more subtil (*phronimôatos*) than any beast of the field" (Gen. iii. I); and our Lord, addressing his apostles, said, "Lo, I send you as sheep in the midst of wolves; be ye, therefore, wise (*phronimoi*) as serpents, and harmless as doves." Yet, as we know, the serpent is not endowed in any special manner with sagacity or reason. The fact is, the epithet "subtil" is applied to the serpent with reference to its form and movements, which convey the abstract idea of subtlety on the same principle that the words "tortuous" and "twisting" have an abstract meaning when we speak of "tortuous policy," or "twisting the meaning of a sentence." Now this subtle entity—this serpent—although presented to Eve in bodily form, was not the less that spirit of evil, the personal existence of which, on the hypothesis that the Scriptures are true, as well as its influence on human minds, must be admitted. Accordingly our first parents were tempted by what St. Paul calls "the wiles (*tas methodeias*) of the devil" (Eph. vi. 11).

Again, the statement in Gen. iii. 6, that "when the woman saw that the tree was good for food, and that it was pleasant to the eyes, and a tree to be desired to make one wise, she took of the fruit thereof, and did eat," is in accordance with what St. John teaches as to "the lust of the flesh," "the lust of the eyes," and "the pride of life," being opposed to "doing the will of God" (I John ii. 16, 17). Also, as we have seen, Adam was associated with a partner, who, having been overcome, in consequence of such desires, by the wiles of Satan, committed sin, and then induced her husband to do the same. Thus, since the world at that time consisted of these two individuals, it is an obvious inference, as well as one of great significance, that Adam was tempted just as all his offspring are—that is, by the world, the flesh, and the devil—and, as all his offspring do, yielded to the temptation.

Although Adam was created in the image of his Maker in respect to being endowed with powers of understanding and reasoning, and although he was made capable of learning and doing righteousness, he was not originally *made righteous*, forasmuch as he sinned: but those whom God makes righteous sin no more, because all the works of God are perfect. "The first man Adam was made a living soul," the breath of life being breathed into his nostrils (Gen. ii. 7). He thus partook of natural life, but not of spiritual life. He was, as St. Paul says, "of the earth, earthy," and all we who are descended from him "bear the image of the earthy" (I Cor. xv. 47, 49). The mind (*to phronêma*) of this natural man is at "enmity with God," and "neither is, nor can be, subject to the law of God" (Rom. viii. 7). This accounts for our perceiving in children from their very infancy a spirit of disobedience, this spirit being derived through natural descent from that which our first parents exhibited in the infancy of the world. The author of the Apocryphal Book, 2 Esdras, writes: "The first man Adam, bearing a wicked heart, transgressed, and was overcome; and so be all they that are born of him" (iii. 21). In the Wisdom of Solomon this passage occurs: "Wisdom preserved the first formed father of the world, that was created alone, and brought him out of his fall" (x. I). But it is to be remarked that the word here translated "fall" is *paraptôma*, the same word that St. Paul uses in Rom. iv. 25 and v. 16, to designate "*our* transgressions." Cruden in his Concordance gives under the word "fall" an elaborate statement of received views respecting "the fall of man," although that word, as the Concordance shows, does not once occur in the Canonical Scriptures in any relation to the sin of Adam.

It is very noteworthy that after the account of Adam's sin in Genesis, no express mention is made of it in subsequent Canonical Books, till we come to the fifth chapter of St. Paul's Epistle to the Romans, where the introduction of sin into the world by *one man* is prominently adduced in an argumentative passage which appears to me to have been much misunderstood.[1] The reason that a fact which is so essential an element in theological systems is so little adverted to in the Scriptures, I consider to be, that these systems have hitherto not recognized an analogy which may be presumed to exist between God's natural creation and His spiritual creation. From what is stated in Genesis i. and ii. there is reason to say that the natural creation was at its beginning without form, and dark, and unfurnished, and that by the power of the Creator, operating, we may presume, according to laws, it was brought into the state of order, light, and adornment (*kosmos*) which we now behold. Hence, arguing from analogy, we might infer that the spiritual creation has its beginning in the reign of sin and death, and that by the power of the Spirit of God, operating according to law on our spirits, it has its consummation in the establishment of righteousness and life.

This analogical inference suffices, I think, to explain why, after the brief initial account of the entrance of sin and death into the world, the purport of the whole of Scripture is to record the

---

[1] See the notes to Rom. v. 12-20, given in pp. 36-38 of my "Translation of St. Paul's Epistle to the Romans" (Cambridge: Deighton and Co, 1871).

subsequent prevalence of sin, and to reveal by what means grace abounded in the gift of righteousness, and how it abounded all the more because the law of sin and death "passed" from one man "upon all men" (Rom. v. 12). The apostle Paul argues that whereas "*death* reigned through one, *much rather* shall they who receive the abundance of grace and of the gift of righteousness reign in *life* through one Jesus Christ" (Rom. v. 17); and in accordance with this doctrine he adds (v. 20), "The law entered by the way (*pareisêlen*) *in order that* the offence might abound, but where sin abounded grace did much more abound." It seems impossible to draw from such sentences as these any other inference than that, according to the scheme of the spiritual creation, the reign of sin and death is the necessary antecedent of the evolution of life from righteousness.

The apostle sums up his argument by saying (v. 19), "For as by the disobedience of one man the many were made sinners, so also by the obedience of one shall the many be made righteous" (*dikaioi katastatêsontai oi polloi*). It is evident that "the many" here includes all that are born in the world, in contradistinction to "the one," Adam, who was created, and from whom all have descended by natural generation. Now, considering that righteousness and life, as necessarily as their opposites sin and death, are related to each other by law as antecedent and consequent, the above revelation that "all will be made righteous" is as direct an assertion of the immortality of all men as could possibly be made. It is, therefore, of the greatest moment, as regards our argument, to ascertain on what grounds we are told that all will eventually be "made righteous" through the obedience of Jesus Christ, and what is the exact meaning of this doctrine. The purpose of this essay will be completely fulfilled if it should be shown that these questions admit of being satisfactorily answered. But before attempting to do this, it is necessary to have a precise understanding of the previous assertion that through Adam's disobedience "the many were made sinners." This preliminary inquiry I now proceed to enter upon.

If we adopt the view expressed in a passage already quoted (2 Esdras iii. 21), we shall, in effect, admit that the transgression of Adam was *the consequence* of his "bearing a wicked heart," and that all who are born of him sin because by *natural generation* they have received from him the same wicked heart. According to this view it must be supposed that "the wicked heart" is in respect to goodness a *tabula rasa*, and that till goodness be formed in it, it is led by natural desires to do evil. Certainly the moral phenomena exhibited by very young children accord with this supposition; and it may reasonably be presumed that St. Paul, in giving to the Romans, to whom he had not personally preached, a synoptical statement of the doctrines he was accustomed to teach, did not set before them the Scriptural account of the introduction and prevalence of sin in any manner not intelligible to ordinary minds from common experience.

What then are we to understand by the assertion that "through the disobedience of one man the many were made sinners"? In answer to this question it is to be said that the word *parakoê* may be taken in this passage to signify "disobedience" abstractedly, and not a special act of disobedience, because *upakoê* in the next clause does not require to be taken in a specific sense, but rather as referring to that holy spirit which was in Jesus Christ, in virtue of which his will was always in subjection to the will of his heavenly Father, and he became "obedient unto death." According to this interpretation, "disobedience" is here put for that wickedness of heart the antecedent existence of which the sin of Adam gave evidence of, and which, by being transmitted from father to son through natural generation, has made all men sinners, to the end that all may be eventually made righteous by spiritual generation.

It is true that the sin of Adam, being the first violation of a command received from God, first made disobedience an objective reality, and that thus sin entered into the world. But although *actual* transgression had this beginning, it does not follow that the *proneness* of the heart of man to transgress was contingent on Adam's sin, or thereby came into existence. On the

13

other hand, it will probably be urged that to ascribe its existence to any other cause is "to make God the author of sin." In answer to this objection it may be said that if it were valid as regards God's moral essence, one might with as good reason urge that it was inconsistent with His power and intelligence that the natural creation should have its beginning in darkness and chaos. However, whether or not this view be accepted, I shall assume that the reality of the natural wickedness of the human heart is admitted, and consequently the remainder of the argument, inasmuch as it has reference to the means by which the wicked heart is subdued and made righteous, will in either case be the same.

The relation of "one" to "many," considered only as a natural fact, is so peculiar and essential an element in the past history and progressive development of the human race, that it might well be supposed to be specially significant with respect to their future destiny; and, in fact, St. Paul has taught us to draw the reasonable inference that whereas through the first Adam the many, by a law from which they cannot rid themselves, have been made sinners, à fortiori through a "second Adam" the many will be made righteous. The course of our argument, consequently, now demands an inquiry as to the means by which the many will be made (katastathêsontai) righteous through the obedience of Jesus Christ. The future tense is particularly to be noticed.

As soon as it was shown by the sin of Adam that the natural man is incapable of obedience to the will of God, a preordained dispensation was begun, whereby the natural man is converted into the spiritual man and made fit for immortality. This dispensation was introduced by a promise, the terms of which could be understood by Adam and Eve after they had learned that the spirit of evil (in whom is "the power of death") through their disobedience brought death into the world. The promise was given in the words "he (autos, Sept.) shall bruise thy head, and thou shalt bruise his heel" (Gen. iii. 15). Hebrew commentators have, I think, rightly taken this passage in the sense—he ("the seed of the woman") shall bruise thee at thy ending, and thou shalt bruise him at his *beginning*. The promise, accordingly, signifies that the power of Satan would prevail *at first*, and for a time, even to putting to death the Son of God (Luke xxii. 53), but that *in the end* that power would by the Son of God be overcome (Luke x. 18). And since with the victory over the spirit of evil an end is put to evil itself, the promise is, in effect, that Adam and his race shall eventually be exempt from death and evil, and partake of a happy immortality.

But in the very next sentence *conditions* are annexed (Gen. iii. 16-19). Because of the imperfection of the natural man, and his opposition, through the subtlety of Satan and the desires of the flesh, to the will of his Maker, labour and sorrow, pain and *death*, were ordained to be his lot, in order that he may *thereby* be made meet to partake of the promise. It is by reason of these conditions that the promise becomes, in effect, a *covenant*, in which of necessity two parties are concerned: God on His part promises happiness and immortality, but to be received only on the above-stated conditions; and man's part is to submit to the conditions, as being ordered by a "faithful Creator," and to look in faith for the fulfilment of the promise. Here, then, are all the essentials of a covenant, excepting *surety* for its fulfilment, which on acknowledged principles of justice might be asked for by man, seeing that he has to satisfy the conditions before he enjoys the benefit. Such security is amply given by God, as will be shown in the sequel of the argument. In short, this covenant admits of being described in terms exactly suited to human covenants, because the providence of God has so ordered these, that, together with other purposes, they answer this, the principal one, of making intelligible the divine covenant. This same covenant might with more exactness be called a *will*, or *testament*, because from its very conditions the benefit it confers cannot be received till after *death* (see Heb. ix. 16, 17). Also, because this covenanted promise runs through the whole of the Scriptures, they have been appropriately named the Scriptures of the Old Testament and of the New Testament, not, however, as signifying that the Old Testament is superseded by the New, but that it reveals an earlier stage of development of the same covenant.

The character and purpose of this covenant began to be unfolded at the threshold of the world's history, on the occasion of offerings being brought to God by Cain and Abel. Abel's offering consisted of "the firstlings of his flock and the fat thereof," and was, therefore, proper for expressing, by visible tokens, the character of the covenant in three essential particulars: first, that it is a covenant of *life*, the animals chosen affording *food*, and that of the choicest kind, for supporting life; secondly, that the covenanted life is entered upon after death, the animals being *slain* for food; thirdly, that pain and death, although, according to law, consequent upon sin, were ordained, not alone for the judicial punishment of sin, the animals that were slain being "*harmless*," but for rendering the spirit of man meet to partake of the future life. Abel was himself in his death the first witness (*martus*) to this truth, and by the same means many chosen servants of God have been "purified and made white" (Dan. xii. 10). The offering of Cain was also proper for food, but as consisting of "fruits of the ground," it was not, like Abel's, susceptible of any meaning relative to the covenant. Grace was given to Abel to select an offering which, as being significant of the covenant, was accepted by God; but the same grace was not given to Cain. "The Lord had respect to Abel and to his offering: but to Cain and to his offering He had not respect."

The narrative goes on to say that because the Lord had not the same respect to Cain's offering as to Abel's, Cain was "very wroth, and his countenance fell," and that on this account he was rebuked. It should be noticed that the terms of the rebuke have no reference to the choice of offering, but to "doing well," implying that Cain's conduct was not "righteous" like that of Abel. To quiet his troubled spirit, he is told that it is God's pleasure that he should stand towards his brother in the relation of protector and ruler. Cain repudiated this relation and slew his brother, acting thus as the unrighteous world, of whom he may be regarded as the representative, have always acted towards God's

16

elect, whom Abel typified. These remarks will afterwards be seen to bear on the general argument.

The distinction which God made between the offerings of Cain and Abel, and His express approval of Abel's offering, might serve to make known, at the time and in succeeding generations, the purport of the promise made originally to Adam, and the ordained conditions of its fulfilment. In fact, the special acceptance by God of Abel's offering may be looked upon as the primary institution of *sacrifice*. The researches of men of learning have abundantly shown that the sacrificing of animals was a very ancient and wide-spread religious practice, but have left altogether unexplained how it *originated*, and whence arose the custom of ratifying a covenant between man and man by *killing* animals; for what reason also the slaying of *innocuous* and *helpless* victims came to be the principal act of religious worship among the Jews, and why it was thought among the Gentiles that such sacrifices *pleased* the gods. These questions do not appear to admit of answers apart from information derived from Scripture. The answers will, I think, be found to be given by what, in reliance on such aid, has been already said, and by what remains to be said, respecting the covenant of immortality. It is quite possible that, as has happened with respect to other practices, that of sacrificing animals was continued long after its original signification ceased to be understood. This may be affirmed of the ratifying of covenants by killing victims (which no sane person nowadays would think of doing), and generally of the sacrifices offered by Gentile nations in honour of their gods, which eventually became mere matters of *custom*, without any distinct appreciation of their intrinsic meaning. In such cases all clue from tradition or history fails, and the explanation of the sources of the practices can be looked for only in the records of Scripture.

It might, however, be questioned whether Abel himself, in making his offering, understood that it had the symbolic meanings ascribed to it above. The answer to this inquiry, given on the authority of what is said in Heb. xi. 4, would seem to be that he did so understand it, inasmuch as it is stated that he brought an acceptable offering *by faith*, and, according to Heb. xi. I, faith may be defined to be an intelligent belief and hopeful expectation of the covenanted life. Also, as bearing on this question, it may be mentioned that in passages of Scripture where Abel is subsequently spoken of (as Matt. xxiii. 85, Heb. xi. 4, I John iii. 12), his *righteousness* is specially referred to. Now, since to do righteousness is to do what is pleasing to God, and, as we are told in Heb. xi. 6, "without faith it is impossible to please God," it follows that Abel's righteousness was the consequence of his faith. In fact, according to St. Paul's teaching, faith and righteousness are by law related to each other as antecedent and consequent (Rom. iii. 27, 28). Consequently we may here draw an inference which forms an essential part of the general argument for immortality. For since we have admitted, as a necessary and self-evident principle, that righteousness is the foundation of immortality, and Scripture presents to us in Abel an instance of the attainment of righteousness by faith, it follows that *faith is a means of partaking of immortality*. This doctrine will be farther treated of in the sequel; but in the mean time it will be well to explain that I consider "righteousness" to consist in obedience by word and deed to the "royal law" according to which, in a perfect social state, every one would do to others as he would that they should do to him. This relation between man and man should, I think, rather be called *righteousness* than *morality*, because the latter word is derived from *mores* (manners), and does not etymologically denote "rectitude," whereas the Greek word for righteousness (*dikaiosunê*) refers to the deciding of what is morally right by a judge, and the office of a judge, as respects social relations, is the highest that men are appointed to discharge towards their fellow men. It should also be noticed that the "faith" I am speaking of does not consist in believing what is not understood, which seems to be a psychological contradiction, but in believing *in consequence of* understanding. "By faith we *understand* that the worlds [or ages (*tous aiônas*)] were framed by the word of God" (Heb. xi. 3). In short, the faith spoken of in Scripture is the basis of all intellectual, as well as of all moral

18

excellence, and is inclusive of what is usually called "talents," or "gifts."

The same covenant, under different typical circumstances, was renewed, first with Noah (Gen. ix. 8-17), and afterwards with Abraham (Gen. xvii. 1-8). The faith of Noah was exhibited not only in building an ark in obedience to God's command, but also in sacrificing clean animals on coming out of the ark. These sacrifices, being offered immediately after the world had been destroyed by the baptism of the Flood, were peculiarly significant of an understanding and acceptance of the covenant of a life to come. After the mention made in the Epistle to the Hebrews of the faith and obedience of which Noah gave evidence by building the ark, it is said of him that "he thereby became heir [inheritor] of the *righteousness* which is according to faith" (Heb. xi. 7). Such righteousness, we have already argued, entitles the possessor of it to immortality.

So also Abraham, when God promised that the land of Canaan should be given to his seed, "builded an altar to the Lord" (Gen. xii. 7, 8), for the purpose, it may be presumed, of sacrificial worship, testifying thus not only belief of the fulfilment of the particular promise, but faith also in the covenanted future life. That Abraham's faith, while he sojourned in Canaan, was directed towards the experience of the world to come, is plainly declared in Heb. xi. 10, where it is asserted that "he looked for a city having foundations, whose builder and maker is God." It was in consequence of such faith that the gift of righteousness was reckoned to him as a *favour*, and "he was called the friend of God" (James ii. 28). Now, the above-mentioned renewal of the covenant was made with Abraham, not solely in respect to his being father of the Hebrew nation, but in respect also to his being typically father of all that believe of all times and nations (compare Gen. xvii. 1-8, with Rom. iv. 11, 16, 17). And all this elect seed receive, in common with their spiritual father, the gift of righteousness through faith—are saved by faith; so that the doctrine that faith is the means whereby the elect are made meet for immortality, which was inferred from the history of Abel, is exemplified in a more comprehensive manner by what is recorded of Abraham.

We have argued above that the patriarchs Noah and Abraham testified their belief and acceptance of the covenant of life by sacrifice. But in the patriarchal times the only surety for the fulfilment of the promise was the direct word of God. With the exception of what is said of Melchisedek, who typified a High Priest to come, no mention is made of the mediation of priests till the priesthood of Aaron was regularly constituted. From that time the priest was mediator between God and the people, and in virtue of his office gave assurance of the fulfilment of the covenant to those who, by offering clean animals for sacrifice, signified their acceptance of its conditions. The priest gave such assurance by mediatorially receiving the offerings, and representing, by sprinkling the blood of the slain animals, *the purifying effect of the suffering of death*. After the ordinances of the law had been instituted, Moses said to the people, "I have set before you life and death: choose life" (Deut. xxx. 19). Seeing that no one can escape the death which is the termination of the present life, this choice between life and death necessarily refers to the covenanted life, the fulfilment of the conditions of which secures from death in the world to come. The author of the Apocryphal Book 2 Esdras, who was wiser, I think, than the author of "The Divine Legation of Moses," has shown that he so understood the passage; for after saying (vii. 48, 44), "The day of doom shall be the end of this time, and the beginning of the immortality for to come, wherein corruption is past, intemperance is at an end, infidelity is cut off, righteousness is grown, and truth is sprung up," he adds (in *v.* 59) with reference to this description of the life to come, "This is the life whereof Moses spake unto the people while he lived, saying, Choose thee life, that thou mayest live."

Sacrifice remained the chief symbol of religious faith up to the time of that great sacrifice of the Son of God, the acceptance of which by the Father sealed the covenant of everlasting life, and made all other sureties sure. The ground of assurance lies in the fact that Jesus Christ in his life and death went through all the experience whereby *our* spirits are formed for immortality. "He learned obedience by the things that he suffered" (Heb. v. 8). He was made perfect "through sufferings" (Heb. ii. 10). "He made him to be sin (*hamartian*; compare Gal. iii. 13) for us, who knew no sin, that we might be made the righteousness of God in Him" (2 Cor. v. 21). Joining with these passages that remarkable one in which Christ is spoken of as "a priest who is made according to the power of an indissoluble (*akatalytou*) life" (Heb. vii. 16), it is evident that our community with him in suffering, in death, and, as we have reason to hope, in resurrection, is ample surety to us for the fulfilment of the covenant of immortality. For as death is the dissolution of life, indissoluble life means exemption from death, and is, therefore, identical with immortality.

That suffering in the flesh is efficacious, as is argued in the foregoing doctrine, towards doing away with sin, may be maintained on the authority both of St. Paul and St. Peter, the former apostle having said, "He that is dead has been justified from sin" (Rom. vi. 7), and the other, "He that has suffered in the flesh has ceased from sin" (I Peter iv. I). But here it is particularly to be noted that this effect is not produced upon *all* who suffer in the flesh. These apostles are speaking of such as have faith; and it is only when suffering is accompanied by a faith which apprehends the covenant of life, and especially lays hold of the surety for its fulfilment given by the suffering and death of the Son of God, that it avails to free from sin. The elect, who through the grace of God have such faith, are drawn by the perfect love, and the *sympathy* in its strictest sense, which were manifested by the obedience unto death of Jesus Christ, to follow the example of his obedience, and thereby to attain to righteousness. By this reasoning it is shown, *but only so far as regards the elect*, that "the many are made righteous by the obedience of Christ." It will in the sequel be argued that the death of Christ has another aspect and a wider effect.

As there was no more occasion for signifying acceptance of the covenant by sacrifice after the sacrifice of Jesus Christ, that form of religious worship came to an end. Thenceforth faith in the covenant was to be expressed by means of symbols which pointed to the sacrifice made once and for all time on the cross. The ordained symbols are *bread* and *wine*, taken in the Lord's Supper. The minister of the Gospel has succeeded to the Jewish priest in respect to giving *surety* officially for the fulfilment of the covenant, and on that account may with propriety be called a *priest.* There is no longer an altar, because the acceptance of the covenant is not, as in the Jewish worship, indicated by sacrifice, but by partaking of *food* in the forms of bread and wine at "the *table* of the Lord." The Christian minister, in delivering these symbols to the worshippers, gives, in virtue of his mediating office, sureties for the fulfilment of the covenant of eternal life; the worshipper who partakes of them in faith receives them as such sureties, and looks for the fulfilment of the covenant. No doubt this office should be discharged by a good and wise minister, who has been regularly appointed thereto; but for the efficacy of the ordinance the chief requisite is *faith* on the part of the recipient—an intelligent faith such as that which has just been mentioned.

The Sacrament of the Lord's Supper is justly regarded as the central ordinance of the Christian religion, and, therefore, of necessity has relation to the means whereby immortality is secured. In fact, in each of the four records of its institution given in Scripture, the word "testament" (*diathêkê*) occurs: in St. Matthew and St. Mark we have, "This is my blood of the New Testament," and in St. Luke and I Cor. xi., "This cup is the New Testament in my blood." What is the meaning of "testament" in these passages, and how is the testament related to the "blood" of Jesus Christ? It is worthy of notice that these questions have received no special consideration in the recent controversies respecting the Lord's Supper, although in order to arrive at the full signification of that ordinance it is clearly necessary to be able to give answers to them. As far as regards the general meaning of the testament, or covenant, its relation to our immortality, and the surety for its fulfilment given by the blood (i.e. the death) of

Jesus Christ, enough, I think, has been said in the foregoing arguments; it remains to inquire, for more complete understanding of the doctrine of the Sacrament, what relations the symbols *bread* and *wine* have to the *Body* and *Blood* of Christ.

"Bread strengthens man's heart," and "wine makes it glad" (Ps. civ. 15). To strengthen the *heart* is to produce confidence. Now, it may be asserted that confidence and joy, being incorporeal entities, are the same in essence under whatever external conditions they are generated. They are the same whether experienced in consequence of taking bread and wine, or in consequence of understanding and accepting the covenant of life made sure by the body and blood of Christ. Although physical science is wholly incapable of informing us *how* the *corporeal* elements bread and wine produce in those who partake of them *feelings* of strength and gladness (the antecedents and consequents not being in the same category), we can yet understand that the Creator of all things might by His immediate will attach to those substances such effects, not alone for the sake of man's body, but for the higher purpose of thereby informing his spirit that there is cause for confidence and joy in the broken body of the Lord, and his poured-out blood. This view is justified by the language of St. Paul, where he says, speaking of the Son of God, that "all things were created through him and *unto* him" (*eis auton*, Col. i. 16); from which doctrine it may be inferred that our Lord, having regard to the cognizable effects of bread and wine spoken of by the Psalmist, said of bread, "This is my body," and of wine, "This is my blood," because his body and blood, when "spiritually discerned," have *the very same effects*.

But why did Christ say, "This *is* my body," "This *is* my blood"? The answer to this question may be given at once by pointing to a rule in Scriptural teaching, according to which the symbol and the thing symbolized are expressed in *identical* terms. The Bible must have been read to little purpose by those who have not discovered that this characteristic pervades all parts both of the Old and the New Testament. On this principle, when

23

speaking to the Jews, our Lord made no distinction between his own body and the visible temple at Jerusalem, just because his body was the proper habitation of the Holy Spirit antecedently to, and comprehensively of, the dwelling of the Spirit in any temple made with hands. St. Paul also employs like teaching where he says, "They are not all Israel that are of Israel" (Rom. ix. 6), the first "Israel" meaning God's elect of all nations and times, and the other the Jewish people, by whom the elect are typified. The rationale of this mode of teaching appears to be, that we could not speak, or even think, of abstract verities, such as that Jesus Christ is to us the author of life, and strength, and joy, without perceptions and feelings antecedently derived from external realities; and the more closely abstractions are viewed by the intervention of their necessary objective antecedents, the more exact and effective will be our knowledge. I venture here to express the opinion that all the contention and diversity of views that have arisen about Transubstantiation and the Real Presence are referable to the non-recognition of the above-mentioned principle of Scriptural teaching by symbols, and generally to an inability to understand and rightly interpret the concrete and symbolic language of Scripture. Defect of knowledge in this respect has given occasion to many errors. With regard to the doctrine of the Sacrament of the Lord's Supper, I am of opinion that the above-mentioned dogmas, and the forms of worship connected with them, which appear to be rightly designated as *superstitious*, have had the effect of very much keeping out of view the relation of that ordinance to the *covenant* which, through the death of Jesus Christ, makes immortality sure. Perhaps it should rather be said that the superstitious practices give evidence that "the blood of the new covenant" is not understood.

From the preceding discussion I draw the conclusion that our Lord, in saying of the wine, "This is my blood of the New Testament," expressed the doctrine that his blood (signifying his death) is both the *pledge* and the means, through faith, of partaking of the joy (signified by the wine) of a new and everlasting life. The Testament is new because it contains the promise of a future inheritance under better sureties than those of the old covenant of the Law.

After having thus considered what the Scriptures say concerning *death*, we have next to inquire what they reveal concerning *resurrection*. As preliminary to this inquiry, it may be remarked that the foregoing arguments relative to Christ's partaking with us in death, are such as point directly to the conclusion that we shall participate with him in resurrection. In St. Paul's teaching (I Cor. xv. 12-19) Christ's resurrection and the resurrection of the dead are events so necessarily related that, "if the dead rise not, Christ was not raised up." But the fact of Christ's resurrection was substantiated by so many witnesses, who saw him alive after his death, that we may with certainty infer, according to this doctrine, that the dead will rise. It is, however, to be observed that the argument of the apostle in the passage just quoted is expressly addressed to those who have faith and knowledge, and cannot be adduced in proof of the doctrine of the resurrection of all men. For evidence as to the truth of this doctrine recourse must be had to other parts of Scripture.

For the present purpose it will suffice to cite two remarkable sayings of our Lord, recorded in St. John's Gospel. He first says, "The hour is coming, and now is, when the dead shall hear the voice of the Son of God: and they that hear shall live" (John v. 25); and then (in *vv.* 28 and 29 of the same chapter) he says, "The hour is coming in which all that are in their graves shall hear his voice, and shall come forth; they that have done good, unto the resurrection of life; and they that have done evil, unto the resurrection of judgment" (*kriseôs*). The first passage refers to a *partial* resurrection, inasmuch as it makes mention of those only who shall hear the voice of the Son of God, and hearing shall live; whereas the other passage asserts that *all* who are in sepulchres (*mnêmeiois*) shall hear his voice, and divides these into two classes—those that have done good, who rise to *live* (the class just before mentioned), and those that have done evil, who rise to be *judged.* The assertion in *vv.* 28 and 29 is, accordingly, a revelation respecting the resurrection of all the dead, and is to be taken as comprehensive of the other; so that the class that will partake of "the resurrection of life" are the same as those of whom it is said in the first passage that they will hear the voice of the Son of God and will *live*. As far as regards the distinction into two classes, this doctrine agrees with that preached by St. Paul, where he affirms that his unbelieving countrymen "themselves allowed that there would be a resurrection of the dead, both of the just and the unjust" (Acts xxiv. 15). It may here be remarked that it is not necessary to infer from its being said in John v. 28, 29, that "all that are in their graves shall hear his voice and come forth," that all will rise *simultaneously*. Rather the separate mention in *v.* 25 of those that hear and live, and especially the assertion that the hour in which *these* hear is not only coming, but "*now is*," would seem to apply exclusively to the resurrection of "the just," and to indicate that this resurrection is antecedent to that of "the unjust." However, to settle this question, which is a very important one, recourse will now be had to other passages of Scripture.

On the principle of regarding, for application in this argument, the *whole* of the Canonical Scriptures as authoritative, it is legitimate to refer to the Book of Revelation for information respecting the resurrection of the dead. Now, in Rev. xx. 5 we have in express terms, "This is the first resurrection." And again, in the next verse, "Blessed and holy is he that hath part in the first resurrection: on such the second death hath no power." It is evident, therefore, that this is the resurrection of the just, and that those who are thus "blessed and holy" are thenceforth exempt from mortality. This conclusion has a very important bearing on our argument; for, on turning to *v.* 4 of the same chapter, we find that the partakers of this resurrection are described as martyrs "who were beheaded for the witness of Jesus, and for the word of God," and generally as those who "received not the mark of the beast on their forehead and on their hand," which may be interpreted as meaning that by intelligent faith and righteous deeds they overcame their spiritual adversaries. It seems, therefore, allowable to infer that this is the company of those who in Scripture are so often called "the elect," who by suffering, experience, and hope, are in this life "sealed" unto the day of redemption (Rev. vii. 2-8, and Eph. iv. 80).

It is, besides, said of these chosen ones that they "lived and reigned with Christ a thousand years," but that "the rest of the dead lived not till the thousand years were finished." It would thus appear that a definite interval of long duration is interposed between the resurrection of the just and the unjust. It is also to be particularly noticed that the seer, speaking of what pertains to that interval of a thousand years during which the spirit of evil is "bound," says that he "saw thrones, and they sat upon them, and judgment was given to them" (Rev. xx. 4). This must refer to the judgment undergone by those who have part in the *first* resurrection, because the rest of the dead do not rise to be judged till the thousand years are ended. As to the elect being judged, the teaching of St. Paul is very explicit, where he says, identifying himself with the general company of the faithful, "We must all appear before the judgment-seat of Christ; that every one may receive the things done through the body, according to what he hath done, whether good or bad" (2 Cor. v. 10. So also Rom. xiv. 10). It is not expressly said in the passage above quoted who they are who sat on thrones and had judgment given to them; but the information is supplied in Matt. xix. 28, where we read, "Jesus said to them [that is, as the context shows, to Peter and the other apostles], Verily I say to you, that ye who have followed me, in the regeneration when the Son of man shall sit on the throne of his glory, ye also shall sit on twelve thrones judging the twelve tribes of Israel." A like revelation, addressed exclusively to the apostles, is given in Luke xxii. 28-80. "The twelve tribes of Israel" is the symbolic designation of the elect—those that are sealed (see Rev. vii. 3-8).

It must now be taken into account that the experience and the deeds of *the present life* alone determine whether any individual is or is not of the number of the elect. Those only who by the favour of God are justified in this life by works done through faith are reckoned among "the just" who partake of the first resurrection. But Scripture nowhere asserts that their spiritual state differs at their resurrection from what it was at the time of their death; rather, it negatives this assumption by describing their state in the interval as that of "*sleep.*" Consequently, not being yet "made perfect," they have need to pass through the judgment just spoken of (compare I Cor. iii. 11-15), in order that by the completion of their *spiritual creation* they might be made meet for immortality. To them, although there is judgment, there is no "*condemnation,*" and, therefore, no "second death." Such, it seems to me, is the Scriptural doctrine of immortality, as far as regards *the elect.*

Before proceeding to speak of the judgment of the whole world, it will be appropriate to consider here what judgment is abstractedly, and what are its purpose and effect. These questions can only be answered by means of what is matter of human experience, and in terms derived therefrom. Now we all know that kings, judges, and magistrates administer justice and judgment for the purpose of making righteousness and truth prevail, and that for the same end they inflict punishment on the guilty. Whatever is this is judgment, and what is not this is not judgment. The portion of the Scriptures which speaks in plainest terms of the object and effect of judgment is, perhaps, that contained in Psalms xcvi., xcvii., xcviii., and xcix. If the words of these Psalms do not refer to the judgment that is to come upon the earth and the whole world in the future age, they will require to be taken in a non-natural sense. But such a sense is here inadmissible, because consistently with what may be inferred, as said above, from *human experience* respecting judgment, namely, that its purpose is to cause righteousness and truth to prevail, this Scripture declares in terms expressive of the highest joy and exultation that for this end the world is judged.

Let us, therefore, now inquire what Scripture reveals respecting the judgment and immortality of the rest of mankind—those who are not numbered among the elect. First, it is clearly implied in Rev. xx. 5, that they live again at the end of the thousand years. Next, as we have already inferred from the words of Christ recorded in John v. 29, they rise to be *judged*. If, as we have argued, it is needful that even the elect should be judged, much rather must judgment overtake the unbelieving and the unrighteous? We are, moreover, expressly told who is to be the righteous Judge: "The Father hath committed all judgment to the Son" (John v. 22). The sinners who, acting "through ignorance" as agents of Satan, arraigned, condemned, and put to death the blameless Son of God, were not alone guilty, inasmuch as it was appointed that they should make manifest and consummate the wickedness that reigns in the heart of the collective world. For this reason Jesus Christ, in fulfilment of a just retribution, is ordained to be Judge of all the world, and of Satan also.

Respecting the *outward means* by which judgment is executed on the ungodly, many things seem to be said in the Book of Revelation; but from being expressed in symbolic language, they are generally "hard to be understood." I shall make no attempt to give explanations of the details of this symbolism, such an inquiry not being necessary for my present purpose; but a few remarks on the contents of the Apocalypse which have a general relation to the purpose and effect of judgment may here be appropriately introduced as bearing on the question of immortality. In the first place, it may be stated that its prophetic language and symbols resemble in so many particulars what we meet with in various parts of the prophecies of the Old Testament, that it might almost be regarded as an epitome of these prophecies. This view is supported by the announcement made in Rev. x. 7, which affirms that, "in the days of the voice of the seventh trumpet, when he shall begin to sound, the mystery of God shall be finished, according to the gospel He declared (*os euêggelise*) unto His servants the prophets" (see also Rev. xxii. 6). It is here to be particularly remarked that after the sounding of six trumpets severally significant of judgment, it is proclaimed that the mystery of God would be finished at the sounding of the seventh and last, this consummation having been antecedently made known as a *gospel* to the Old Testament prophets. This text accordingly agrees with the tenor of the argument previously adduced respecting the final effect of judgment in establishing the reign, so much to be desired, of truth and righteousness. At the end of the judgment "the temple of God is opened in heaven, and there is seen in His temple the ark of His covenant" (Rev. xi. 19). This is the covenant of immortality, which, having been originally made (as has already been indicated) with Adam after his transgression, was afterwards renewed with Noah and with Abraham, was represented by symbols and proclaimed orally by Moses in the wilderness, and, finally, was confirmed by the sacrifice of Jesus Christ.

Equally remarkable is another revelation, which tells us that the elect, the one hundred and forty-four thousand who have been made perfect by the experience they have gone through in the thousand years of the first resurrection, are joined with the Son of God in the execution of the general judgment. In Rev. xix. 14, it is said that "the armies in heaven followed him upon white horses, clothed in fine linen, white and clean." This clothing proves that the attendant army consisted of the saints made perfect in righteousness, as will be evident by comparing *vv.* 7 and 8 of the same chapter. In *v.* 15 it is asserted respecting "The Word of God," that "he shall rule the nations with a rod of iron;" and he says himself, speaking of his faithful followers, "To him that overcometh and keepeth my works unto the end will I give power over the nations; and he shall rule them with a rod of iron" (Rev. ii. 26, 27). Also we have in Psalm cxlix. 6-9, "Let a two-edged sword be in their hand, to execute vengeance upon the nations, punishments upon the peoples; to bind their kings with chains, and their rulers with fetters of iron; to execute upon them the judgment written: this honour have all His saints." Moreover, St. Paul writes to the Corinthians: "Do ye not know that the saints shall judge the world?" "Know ye not that we shall judge angels?" In short, the doctrine of Scripture on this prerogative of the saints is very explicit.

Again, it is uniformly affirmed in Scripture that every one will be judged "according to his works." Of course, "words" are included in "works;" for our Lord said expressly, "Every idle word that men shall speak, they shall give account thereof in the day of judgment; for by thy words thou shalt be justified, and by thy words thou shalt be condemned" (Matt. xii. 86, 87). It would seem that the judgment, as being conducted by *external* means, takes account of human *thoughts* only so far as their consequences are manifested by overt deeds and spoken words. It is not the less true, according to the doctrine of the Lord himself (in Mark iv. 22, and Luke viii. 17), that in the day of judgment all secret and hidden things will be revealed. The words in St. Mark, "neither was anything kept secret but in order that (*hina*) it should come abroad," seem expressly to indicate the relation in which things hidden in the present age stand to the revelations of that day. St. Paul also writes to the Romans, speaking of them who have not received the law by direct communication: "They show the work of the law written in their hearts, their conscience bearing them witness, and their thoughts, one with another, accusing, or also excusing, in the day when God shall judge the secrets of men, according to my gospel, through Jesus Christ" (Rom. ii. 15, 16). (This, I think, should be the translation of the passage.) It may be noticed that here again "gospel" is mentioned in connection with "judgment."

Now, the very terms, "judgment according to works," imply that the works brought into judgment are not all equally bad, and that there may be both "good and bad;" which also may be inferred from the passage just quoted from the Epistle to the Romans. In fact, it is not too much to assume that all the deeds and experience of the present life are contributory in different ways to the final purpose of the judgment. We have already argued, in accordance with what is said in 2 Cor. v. 10, that the saints will be judged according to their works, and from I Cor. iii. 11-15, we learn that their works will be tried by fire, but they themselves will be saved, "yet so as by fire." We have now to enter upon the important inquiry as to whether Scripture reveals an analogous dispensation with respect to the rest of mankind.

Hard as it may be for us to conceive by what means the deeds and experience of all men, the living and the dead, will be brought under review in the day of judgment, that so it will be is undoubtedly the teaching of Scripture. Our understanding of this wonderful event may perhaps be assisted by taking into account what St. Paul said to the Athenians: "In Him we live, and move, and have our being;" whence it may be inferred that all our works and words, and even feelings and thoughts, are known to God. With reference to this question, it would, I think, be legitimate to call to our aid the knowledge of the external creation, which has been so largely extended in the present day. After long attention given to the acquisition of such knowledge, I seem to see that it points to the conclusion that all the forces of nature are resident in a universal aetherial medium, extending through all space, and pervading all visible and tangible substances, by the intervention of which all power is exerted, whether it be by the immediate will of God, or mediately, by that of angels or of men. (I assume that there can be no exertion of power apart from the will and consciousness of an agent.) Consequently the Spirit of the Universe must be cognizant of every exertion of power and of its effects. To this consideration another of peculiar significance is to be added. The faculty which we possess to a limited extent, depending on bodily conditions and organization, of *remembering* the consequences of exerted power, whether as operating ourselves, or being operated upon, must be conceived of as pertaining, without any limitation, to the Creator of the aetherial substance and the Source of all power. In this manner it seems possible to understand how all actions and all events may be written down (speaking metaphorically) in the Book of God's *remembrance*, and so be brought into judgment.

The universality and the character of the future judgment are declared in Rev. xx. 11-13, with particular reference to the presence and majesty of "One who sat on a great white throne," who, doubtless, is God the Father, the Creator of heaven and earth. The seer says in this passage, "I saw the dead, small and great, stand before God; and the books were opened: and another book was opened, which is the book of life: and the dead were judged out of those things which were written in the books, according to their works." The mention made of "the books" indicates that what is here said of the general judgment pertains exclusively to God the Father, by whose almighty power and omniscience, as I have endeavoured to show in the preceding paragraph, all the deeds and experience of the present life are held in remembrance to be brought under judgment. But it would be an error to suppose that this general judgment is different from that the process and results of which, as effected through the Son of man and his attendant armies, are symbolically described in previous parts of the Apocalypse. The judgment was ordained by decree of the Father, and prearranged by His wisdom, and in accordance therewith it is executed by the Son, who, apparently on this account, speaks thus of himself: "To him that overcometh will I give to sit with me in my throne, as I also overcame and sat with my Father in His throne" (Rev. iii. 21). This throne which the Son shares with the Father may be presumed to be the seat of power exercised in judgment (compare Rev. ii. 26, 27). Why "the book of life" is mentioned in connection with the books from the contents of which the dead are judged, will be shown in the sequel of the argument.

There are other considerations relating to the future judgment which it is necessary to enter into in order to complete the argument for the immortality of all men. We live in a world in which sorrow and pain and death abound everywhere and at all times, and although these are actual consequences of sin, inasmuch as they would be non-existent if sin did not antecedently exist, it is not the less true that the *law* which in the present time of imperfection connects suffering with sin, tends in its operation towards bringing on eventually a state of perfection. Thus there is a final cause for that law. I have already (page 14) illustrated this doctrine by reference to the process whereby the actual condition and adornment of this earth were elaborated by the operation of physical laws out of a state of darkness and chaos. This view is corroborated by the noticeable fact that suffering in this life, whether caused by the three scourges, war, pestilence, and famine, or what we call accident, or by the injustice and cruelty of men, by no means in proportion to guilt, since even the innocent thereby sometimes suffer. Now, as all human deeds and experience are taken cognizance of in the great day of judgment, it must be admitted that sufferings of the kind just mentioned will be included in the account. In what way, and with what effect, will, I think, be to some extent indicated by the following considerations.

Besides the principle of animal life (*psyche*) which man partakes of in common with the creatures of a lower order, there is within him a spirit (*pneuma*) which is being formed, educated, and built up, all the time that it is the tenant of a corporeal "vessel." On account of this law of progressiveness, the spirit of a child, as we can all see, differs in its feelings and its understanding from that of a man. In short, spirit perfected is the principle of immortal life. Now, during our waking hours our spirits are replete with consciousness and thought, which, however, at the moment of falling asleep depart from us. The spirit is then taken into the keeping of the angels of God, to be by them restored into its place in the body at the moment of waking up and of return to consciousness. In like manner at death the spirits of all men, good and wicked, pass into the custody of the Creator of spirits, to wait for the return to consciousness by being on the morning of their resurrection again united with body,—not, however, with the same natural body, but with a spiritual body (I Cor. xv. 44). The union of spirit with bodily essence appears to be a necessary condition of human consciousness, and to have been ordained for the special reasons that we are destined to live hereafter not only individually, but in *social* relations also, and that only through the medium of body is there communion between one man's spirit and that of another.

This being understood, it is next to be observed that in the forming and building up ("edification") of spirit, the human *will* is concerned, and that, according to a man's choice of action, his spirit may be educated for being good or for being wicked, may be sanctified or defiled. There is, in short, no act or experience in human life which in this respect is indifferent. But what the spirit is thus made during its passage through this life, such it is when it is taken into the hands of its Creator, and such, as we may conclude from the teaching of Scripture and from its having in the mean time existed apart from body, it will be, with all its imperfections, on the day of its resurrection. It has already been maintained that, because of imperfection, it is necessary that even the elect should be judged, to the end that by this means their spirits may be made perfect. But our concern now is with the effect of judgment on those who are not of the number of the elect. For the purpose of illustrating what I am about to say on this head, I shall begin with making an application of the argument in a particular instance.

I have recently seen it stated, among the news of the day, that it is the practice of a barbarous African king to cut off the heads of twelve or more of his subjects, merely to pay a compliment to a distinguished visitor. Are we to think that this transaction both begins and ends here? Although we have no ground for asserting that the victims in this case are to be counted among God's elect, inasmuch as they must be supposed to be devoid of the faith and righteousness which are necessary to constitute a title to that high privilege, we may yet believe that the bodily suffering they endured was contributory to the formation of their spirits for their future destiny. If even those who have "understanding"—elect saints—have undergone sufferings and been "beheaded" in order that thus they might be "purified and made white," (compare Dan. xi. 33-35, and xii. 10, with Rev. xx. 4), why should we not believe that the sufferings of those poor Africans, who are equally children of God, had like effect? That suffering is in this manner efficacious is proved by the sacrifice of the Son of God on the cross, who, after having proved by his miracles that he had all human ills under control, *voluntarily* submitted to be made perfect by enduring shame and pain, that thus he might both exemplify and justify the ways of God in the creation of immortal spirits. This sacrifice is a full and sufficient explanation of all the evil in the world. When, therefore, in the time of the resurrection of the unjust the slayer and the slain, in this instance, appear before the judgment-seat of God, and are condemned, as not being among those who are saved in the first resurrection, to undergo the second death, is it not reasonable to conclude that the tribulation and pain of that event will fall much more heavily on the murderer than on those he slew, and that the punishment and sufferings that have still to be endured in order that the final purpose of the judgment may be accomplished, will be inflicted with far greater severity on him than on them? (See on this point what is said concerning the future judgment in the Wisdom of Solomon vi. 3-6.)

On this principle many apparent anomalies in the present age of the world admit of explanation. Why, for instance, is so large a proportion of mankind condemned, irrespective of their deserts, to be poor, and to labour with their hands in anxiety for the maintenance of themselves and their families? We have reason from Scripture to say that such conditions of life, if united with the *faith* that looks for better things to come, may be counted among means ordained by God for preparing the spirits of His elect for their destined inheritance ("Hate not laborious work, neither husbandry, which the Most High hath ordained" [Ecclesiasticus vii. 15]). And where such faith is absent, may we not still say that conditions of the present life to which the great mass of mankind are subject must be contributory to forming their spirits for their future existence? Leaving out of consideration who are the elect, and who not, which God only knows, can we think that the patience of the labourer and artisan, the endurance of the seafaring man, and the devotedness of the soldier, who at the call of duty, and in spite of the promptings of self-preservation, exposes himself to almost certain death on the field of battle, have no relation to their future destiny? As regards, especially, the spirit of self-sacrifice of the soldier, so opposed to all the calculations of personal interest, it seems to me that the desire of glory, or the expectation of reward, will not wholly account for it, but rather that it is indicative of there being in the warrior's breast an undefined conviction that he better fulfils the purpose of life by braving a painful death than by living at home in ease. It is worthy of remark that although in Scripture war is spoken of as a calamity, the occupation of a soldier is nowhere condemned, but is rather commended on account of its disciplinary effect and abstractedness from the affairs of life (see 2 Tim. ii. 3, 4). It should be observed that the different kinds of human experience adverted to above are all supposed to stand apart from personal acts done in violation of the dictates of *conscience*. Such acts will doubtless be tried by the course of the general judgment, and will have effect in the condemnation of the offenders, and in punishment awarded according to the guiltiness of their deeds.

The calamities of human life may be put generally under the two heads of "tribulation" and "slaughter"—different kinds of sorrow and trouble, and different kinds of death. These constitute the groaning and travailing of the whole creation unto the time being (*a chri tou nun*), spoken of by St. Paul in Rom. viii. 22 and called in St. Mark xiii. 8, the beginnings of sorrows (*ôdinôn*). But in the time of the world to come, the same forms of suffering have their consummation and ending. In Rev. vii. 14, mention is made of "*the* great tribulation," and at the same time of "a countless multitude who come out of it." This can be no other than that "great tribulation" respecting which our Lord said, according to St. Matt. xxiv. 21, that it will be "such as was not since the beginning of the world to this time, *nor ever shall be*," and according to St. Mark xiii. 19, that "those days shall be affliction such as was not from the beginning of the creation which God created unto this time, *neither shall be*." The identity of the events spoken of in the Gospels and in the Apocalypse may also be inferred from the words *cheimônos* (tempest-time) and *sabbatô* (on the sabbath) contained in Matt. xxiv. 20, the former referring to the storm of indignation and wrath which proceeds from "the Lamb" when he comes to execute Judgment, and the latter to the time in which the judgment takes place, which is designated the sabbath, or seventh day, as following upon the termination of the present age of the world, and also as being that sabbath of which, as said in Luke vi. 5, "the Son of man is Lord."

Again, in proof of the doctrine that the process, or effect, of the general judgment is characterized in Scripture as "slaughter," Isa. xxxiv. 1-6 may be cited, it being said in that passage that "the indignation of the Lord is upon all nations," that "he hath delivered them to the slaughter," and in connection therewith that "all the host of heaven shall be dissolved, and the heaven shall be rolled together as a scroll" (compare Rev. vi. 18-14). Of the same import is the prophecy in Rev. xiv. 14-20, at the end of which the treading of "the great winepress of the wrath of God" is described in terms closely agreeing with those in Isa. lxiii. 1-4. We have, besides, the remarkable passage, Rev. xix. 17-21, which represents the fowls of heaven as being called together to feast on the flesh of the slain, after great slaughter had been wrought by "the sharp sword" which proceeds out of the mouth of him who is called "The Word of God." This sword represents the cutting and destructive effect of the words of judgment and condemnation which the Son of God will pronounce on sinners when he comes to judge the whole world. It is not necessary for my purpose to interpret particularly the symbolism contained in the passages just quoted; it suffices to draw from them the general inference that, as regards *all* men, trouble and pain and death in the present age of the world are the beginnings of an Œconomy for forming spirits for immortality, which is destined to be consummated in the age to come.

To complete the argument from Scripture it only remains now to take into consideration those passages which expressly reveal the effect of the general judgment, and to ascertain what relation the revelations have to the question of immortality. These passages are of two kinds, some being composed entirely of symbolic language requiring interpretation, while others are expressed in terms that may be readily understood. The former must be supposed to admit of being interpreted consistently with the plain meaning of the other kind. Accordingly, for the purpose above mentioned, I proceed now to offer an interpretation of Rev. xx. 11-15, this passage evidently giving a synoptical account, in symbolic terms, of the process and the effect of the general judgment.

I have already adverted (p. 48) to the contents of *vv.* 11 and 12, so far as they refer to the Person of the Judge, and to His judging the dead, according to their works, "out of the things written in the *books.*" "The great *white* throne" (*v.* 11) is evidently the seat of righteous judgment. The inspired writer, in order to account for his seeing in vision the dead, "small and great, standing before the throne," reveals, besides, that "the sea gave up the dead that were in it, and Death and Hades gave up the dead that were in them" (*v.* 13). Now, the context hardly allows of taking "the sea" here in its literal objective sense, requiring rather the interpretation that the natural sea symbolizes by its invisible depths the incognizable state of the dead before resurrection. In the "new heaven and earth," which is the end of all creation, "sea exists no longer" (Rev. xxi. 1). Hades, as apparently might be inferred from the proper sense of the word, signifies that invisible state of departed spirits which, as just said, is symbolized as being concealed in the depths of "the sea," and also, as I have already pointed out, has to death a necessary relation of sequence ("Hades followed with him" [Rev. vi. 8]). This explains why Death and Hades are represented as a conjoint power having possession of the dead. In Rev. i. 18, as well as in Rev. vi. 8, they are mentioned in close connection, and in the latter passage power is said to be given to them in common.

I take occasion to make some remarks here on I Peter iii. 19, as the sense of this passage might be thought to be contradictory to the meaning assigned above to Hades. It affirms that "in spirit Christ went and preached to the spirits in custody (*en phylakê*)." Now, the literal meaning of the concrete terms, "went and preached" (*poreutheis ekêruxen*), is *excluded* by "in spirit" going before, and they consequently require an abstract interpretation. It has already been argued (p. 50) that the word "custody" applies

39

to departed spirits in the sense of their being in the *keeping* of the Creator of spirits; whence it follows that "spirits in custody" and "spirits in Hades" have the same meaning. But neither of these expressions signifies anything as to *locality*, for the simple reason that locality cannot be predicated of spirit apart from body. The abstract interpretation of the passage of St. Peter may, I think, be reached by the following argument. The word *ekêruxen* above cited is not that ordinarily used with respect to preaching the Gospel, and therefore it is the more to be noticed that where Noah is called "a preacher of righteousness" (2 Peter ii. 5), the Greek word is *kêruka*. May we not hence infer that Noah, by "the spirit of Christ" which was in him (compare I Peter i. 11), preached to the unbelieving and "disobedient" of his day, and that their spirits, although the world in which they lived was so long since destroyed by the Flood, are, together with all other departed spirits, still in God's custody, to be hereafter raised up and judged? We are farther informed respecting Noah's preaching, which consisted apparently of deeds rather than of words, that "by preparing an ark for the saving of his house, he condemned the world, and became heir of the righteousness which is according to faith" (Heb. xi. 7).

We have now to inquire what interpretation may be given to the symbolic language (in Rev. xx. 14) which affirms that "Death and Hades were cast into the lake of fire," and that "this is the second death, the lake of fire." The first mention of the lake of fire occurs in Rev. xix. 20, where it is described as "burning with brimstone," and both "the beast," and "the false prophet" associated with him (*ho met autou*), are said to be "cast alive" into this lake. But the rest (*oi loipoi*), namely, "the kings of the earth and their armies, gathered together to make war against him who sat on the horse and against his army," were slain by the sword that proceeds out of his mouth, that is, by the sharp and searching words of righteousness and truth, whereby he, "The Word of God," judges and pronounces condemnation in the last day (compare John xii. 48). In Rev. xx. 7-10, we are farther told that Satan, after being let loose from prison at the end of the thousand years when "the rest of the dead" live again (v. 5), and after collecting together all the *risen* nations of the earth, "the number of whom is as the sand of the sea" (v. 8), leads them to their destruction in battle against the God of heaven, and is himself "cast into the lake of fire and brimstone, where are the beast and the false prophet" (v. 10). Consequently, "Satan," who is opposed to God the Father, the God of heaven, "the beast," which, as signifying the spirit of the world, is opposed to the Holy Spirit, and "the false prophet," who is the symbolic representative of all *anti-Christian* power objectively opposed to the Son of God, are all three cast into a lake of fire "*burning with brimstone.*" But of Death and Hades it is only said that they were cast into a lake of fire. Their being cast into the depths of "a lake" signifies that they become incognizable entities, and "lake of fire" indicates that they remain such by an irreversible law, fire being the symbol of force of law (see Deut. xxxiii. 2). For this reason "the lake of fire" is put in apposition (in *v.* 14) with "the second death," which is the extinction of death. Now, Satan, the beast, and the false prophet, being regarded as *personal* existences motived by *will*, and in that respect unlike Death and Hades, are cast not simply into a lake of fire, but into a lake burning with brimstone, which apparently signifies that from the time these "adversaries" cease to have cognizable existence, their antecedent power and influence will be regarded by those who were once subject to them with antipathy and abhorrence, so that any return to the same subjection will (as we say) be morally impossible. When in the end God has become "all in all," no antagonism remains; all enemies have been subdued. Any one who is unwilling to accept the foregoing interpretation might reasonably be asked in what other way he can explain why, of all created things, *brimstone* is specially mentioned with reference to this "mystery" (see Rev. xvii. 5, 16).

In the last verse of the passage under consideration we have, "And if any one (*ei tis*) was not found written in the book of life, he was cast into the lake of fire" (v. 15). It is to be observed that the lake of fire is not here said to be burning with brimstone.

41

This sentence must accordingly receive an interpretation analogous to that given above with respect to Death and Hades. When the final judgment has had complete effect, there will no longer be objective existence of any whose names are not in the book of life, because all will have been made meet for the inheritance of life. For this reason "the book of life" is mentioned (in *v.* 12) in immediate connection with the books containing the records according to which the judgment is transacted. I am well aware that the preceding interpretations do not accord with views entertained by many in the present day. I remember to have heard a sermon on the text, "This is the second death," in the course of which the preacher did not once advert to the word "This," but gave a description, the most terrible his imagination could supply, of what he judged to be the second death. We find revealed in Scripture respecting "the terrors of the Lord"—the anguish and tribulation, the slaughter and destruction, proceeding from His wrath in the day of judgment—quite enough to deter sinners from going on in sin, without gratuitously adding the doctrine of the perpetuity of evil, the preaching of which seems to have the effect of hindering the belief and expectation of the impending realities of that great day. Besides, it may well be asked how such preaching can be reconciled with the Gospel revelations, stated in language devoid of symbol, which are contained in Rev. xxi.; to which I shall afterwards have occasion to call attention. But, first, it will be necessary to inquire what is the doctrine of Scripture respecting future "punishment" and "torment."

On proceeding to this part of the argument it will be proper to revert to a principle which has already been admitted as self-evident (p. 9), namely, that a state of perfect righteousness and a happy immortality are so essentially and necessarily related that one cannot subsist without the other. It is, however, to be said that this doctrine is nowhere expressed in such words in Scripture. In fact, the abstract terms, "essentially and necessarily related," are altogether unlike any Scriptural mode of expression. Yet it may be that the truth which we think we understand when we express it in such terms may admit of being *extracted* in a more definite form from the concrete language of Scripture; and, in order that our argument for immortality may be shown to rest entirely on a Scriptural foundation, I shall now endeavour to show that this is the case with respect to the above-stated doctrine, by citing and discussing various passages of the Old and New Testament.

In the first place, I remark that righteousness and salvation, righteousness and peace, are so often and in such manner mentioned together in the word of God, that we may thence infer that, according to a law of the Divine (Economy, personal righteousness is a condition necessarily antecedent to salvation (safety) and peace (see Ps. xxiv. 5, and lxxxv. 7-18; Isa. xlv. 7, 8, xlvi. 18, li. 5, lxii. I, and many like passages). For, on the other hand, it is twice expressly declared that God has said, "There is no peace to the wicked" (Isa. xlviii. 22, and lvii. 21). So in Rev. xiv. it is affirmed respecting sinners (who are comprehensively described as those who worship the beast and his image, and receive the mark of his name on the forehead or the hand—in their beliefs or their deeds) that "they have no rest day nor night" (*vv.* 9 and 11). Of the same sinners it is also declared that "they shall drink of the wine of the wrath of God, which is poured out without mixture into the cup of his indignation; and shall be tormented with fire and brimstone in the presence of the holy angels, and in the presence of the Lamb" (v. 10). The fire of the torment is the operation of the holy law of righteousness which they have broken, and the brimstone by the offensiveness of its smoke represents the self-condemnation and reproach of conscience with which they are tormented when their sins are laid bare in the presence of the holy angels and of the *Lamb*, who by reason of their sins was slain. Lastly, we are told that "the smoke of their torment ascendeth up for ever and ever." The general signification of "smoke," regarded as a symbol, appears to be, effect or consequence. Thus, in the remarkable symbol of "a smoking furnace" seen in vision by Abraham (Gen. xv. 17), the fire of the furnace may represent the operation of the law, and the smoke may symbolize "the abounding" of the sins of mankind consequent upon that operation (see Rom. v. 20; also compare 2 Esdras iv. 48). But in the passage before us we have "smoke of torment," of which smoke it is said that it "ascends up for ever and ever," signifying, it would seem, the perpetuity of the *effect* of the torment. This interpretation accordingly agrees with that previously given (p. 61) relative to "the lake of fire burning with brimstone." There is, however, this difference to be noted, that whereas the present passage relates especially to the effect of the *pain and torment* attendant upon the *process* of being judged, the other speaks of the effect of the second *death* to which the wicked, after being tried by the judgment, are condemned.

The portion of Scripture contained in Matt. xxv. 31-46, gives, concerning the awards to be respectively adjudged to the righteous and unrighteous, and the final consequences of the judgment, certain revelations, symbolically expressed, which are made by the Lord himself, the future Judge. In order to complete the argument from Scripture respecting the effect of judgment, we must endeavour to interpret these revelations. "When the Son of man shall come in his glory, and all the holy angels with him, he will sit on the throne of his glory: and all nations will be gathered before him: and he will separate them one from another, as a shepherd separates the sheep from the goats; and he will place the sheep on his right hand, and the goats on his left" (*vv.* 31-33). We are thus told that all of all nations will come into the presence of the Judge, and that he will separate them into two portions, as distinct the one from the other as sheep are from goats. From what is said farther on we gather that one portion are "the just" (*oi dikaioi, v.* 37), and the other the unjust; but no mention is made of a particular process of separation. Consequently there is nothing here which contradicts the conclusion before arrived at (p. 38), that the just are separated from the unjust by partaking of the first resurrection; rather, that conclusion is in accordance with this revelation respecting the place of honour "on the right hand" being assigned to the just, and their being prepared to receive it when the whole assembly, just and unjust, are gathered together before the Judge. In *v.* 34, as also in *v.* 40, the Judge is called "the King" (*ho Basileus*), forasmuch as he is "the faithful and true" One, who "in righteousness judges and makes war," and to whom belongs in a special manner the title of "King of kings and Lord of lords" (see Rev. xix. 11, 16).

We have next to consider the statements of the grounds on which the awards are made, which are very remarkable. "Then shall the King say to them on his right hand, Come, ye blessed of my Father, inherit the kingdom prepared for you from the foundation of the world. For I was hungry, and ye gave me meat; I was thirsty, and ye gave me drink; I was a stranger, and ye took me in; naked, and ye clothed me; I was sick, and ye visited me; I was in prison, and ye came to me. Then shall the righteous answer him, saying, Lord, when saw we thee hungry, and fed thee? or thirsty, and gave thee drink? When saw we thee a stranger, and took thee in? or naked, and clothed thee? Or when saw we thee sick, or in prison, and came unto thee? And the King shall answer and say to them, Verily I say to you, Inasmuch as ye have done it unto one of the least of these my brethren, ye have done it unto me" (*vv.* 84-40). What is chiefly noteworthy in these words is, that the Judge identifies himself with suffering humanity, and accounts as "brethren" even "the least" of those that suffer, having, when he "dwelt among us," participated in the toils and afflictions to which sinful man is subject (although "in him was no sin)," and submitted in the end to the shame and pain of dying on the cross, although he had shown by his miracles that he had power over death and all the ills of humanity. As is written in Isaiah liii. 4, "He hath borne *our* griefs and carried *our* sorrows." This the Son of God voluntarily took upon himself out of love and compassion towards us, knowing that, by ordinance of his Father, the Creator of spirits, "we must through many tribulations enter into the kingdom of God" (Acts xiv. 22), and be made heirs of immortality, and that consequently we had need of such assurance of obtaining the appointed inheritance as that which is given by his partaking with us of life, death, and resurrection (see what is said on this part of the subject in p. 29).

Besides this, the sympathy of Jesus Christ with human suffering, which was also shown by his miracles of healing, is specially a reason for giving *practical* proof, by acts of benevolence and mercy towards our fellow men, that we partake of the same spirit. It is with reference to such *outward* evidence of faith and righteousness, that the decision of the Judge, given in the passage above quoted, is pronounced. It seems, too, from the questions put to the Judge by the company of the righteous, and the answer they received, that their acts of kindness and mercy, done in humility and faith, were accepted by the Judge, out of his sympathy and community with the sufferers, as done to himself, although the doers had not had previous knowledge or expectation that their good deeds would be so accepted.

The sentence pronounced on the unrighteous, and the reasons for it, are thus stated in *vv.* 41-45: "Then shall he say also to them on the left hand, Depart from me, ye cursed, into the Œonian fire (*to pur to aiônion*, i.e. the fire of judgment in the future *aiôn*) prepared for the devil and his angels: for I was hungry, and ye gave me no meat; I was thirsty, and ye gave me no drink; I was a stranger, and ye took me not in; naked, and ye clothed me not; sick, and in prison, and ye visited me not. Then shall they also answer him, saying, Lord, when saw we thee hungry, or athirst, or a stranger, or naked, or sick, or in prison, and did not minister unto thee? Then shall he answer them, saying, Verily, I say to you, inasmuch as ye did it not to one of the least of these, ye did it not to me." It should be noticed that the terms of this award are the exact contraries of those of the award to the righteous. On the one hand, the King says, "Come, ye blessed of my Father, inherit the kingdom prepared for you from the foundation of the world;" on the other, he says, "Depart from me, ye cursed, into the Œonian fire prepared for the devil and his angels;" and the account of what the Judge further says to the unrighteous, and of what they say to him, although somewhat briefer than that relating to the righteous, is made up of exactly opposite particulars. On this principle, since the decision respecting the righteous is pronounced on the grounds of positive works of righteousness done in humility and faith, that respecting the unrighteous has regard only to the *omission* to do such works through presumption and unbelief. The same exhibition of opposite circumstances and qualities, and the same principle of condemnation for sins of omission exclusively of those of commission, are observable in the two other symbolic representations contained in the same chapter—the parable of the ten virgins, and the parable of the talents. In short, the general purport of the chapter is to indicate, that in the sight of the righteous Judge sins of omission, not less than sins of commission, demand condemnation and punishment; the reasons for which appear to be that both kinds are equally violations of the royal law, "Thou shalt love thy neighbour as thyself" (James ii. 8), and perfect obedience to this law is the necessary foundation of a *common* immortality.

It only remains now to speak of the final issue of the judgment stated thus in *v.* 46: "And these shall go away into eternal punishment, but the righteous into external life." It must be admitted that the first clause of this sentence, taken as it is usually taken, expresses the perpetuity of evil, inasmuch as "punishment" is an evil. But after this has been conceded, there is still something more to be said on this doctrine. It is evident from the context that by "these" is meant the ungodly just before spoken of, who, having shown, by their neglecting to give proof of love towards their neighbours, that the love of God is not in them (see I John iv. 20), are counted as enemies, and as such must be punished. For there is no neutral position: all who do not obey the commands of Christ are opposed to him, and all that is opposed to him is destined to be brought under subjection. Further, it is to be noticed that although the final decision is expressed generally in accordance with the before-mentioned principle of employing exactly opposite terms relatively to the righteous and the wicked, here the opposite of "eternal life" is "eternal punishment," and not "eternal death," the latter expression being nowhere found in Scripture. May it not hence be argued that, as among men the punishment of the guilty has not for its purpose the infliction of pain and penalty, but rather is the means employed to the end that laws may be obeyed, so the end of divine punishment is for correction, and for giving effect to and establishing the law of universal righteousness. If it should hence be inferred that the word "eternal" is applied to future punishment with reference to that permanence of *effect* which, as has already been indicated (p. 65), is symbolically represented by the perpetual ascent of "the smoke of torment," against this inference it might reasonably be urged that "eternal" ought to be taken in the same sense relatively to the "punishment" of the wicked, as relatively to the "life" of the righteous, and eternity is here predicated of the one just as of the other. Now, although this reasoning appears to be irrefragable, the additional arguments from Scripture which I am about to adduce will, I think, show that there must be some other way of regarding the doctrine of future punishment, which, although not inconsistent with that to which the foregoing interpretation of Matt. xxv. 46 has conducted, differs from it either as to point of view or comprehensiveness.

In the first place, it is to be observed that in our Lord's discourses doctrine was very generally taught by parables and symbolic language, which required to be interpreted in order that the abstract and spiritual truths thereby conveyed might be understood. (This remark applies to the whole of the passage, Matt. xxv. 31-46, brought under review in the foregoing discussion.) In Mark iv. 34, it is said that "without a parable he spake not to them," that is, to the multitude, and that "in private he explained all things to his disciples." Being asked by the disciples, when he was preaching to a great multitude assembled together on the sea-shore to hear him, why he spake to them in parables, he answered, "Because it is given to you to know the mysteries of the kingdom of heaven, but to them it is not given. For whosoever hath, to him it shall be given, and he shall have more abundance; but whosoever hath not, from him shall be taken away even that he hath. Therefore speak I to them in parables, because seeing they see not, and hearing they hear not, neither do they understand" (Matt. xiii. 10-13). It is here affirmed that although parables from their very character are expressed in terms which the use of the senses renders intelligible, there are those who do not or will not understand them, who for this reason, on the principle of not giving to those who have not, are spoken to only in parables, so that they continue in ignorance. As every effect or consequence implies the antecedence of the *purpose* of an agent, with respect to this consequence we find it stated in Luke viii. 10, that our Lord expressly addressed the disciples in these words: "Unto you it is given to know the mysteries of the kingdom of God, but to the rest in parables, *that seeing they may not see, and hearing they may not understand.*" To a selected few is granted the favour of being able to discern, *through the objective sense* of parables, the interior signification whereby mysteries of the kingdom of God are revealed, whilst from the rest—the multitude—although the objective sense is the same to them as to the others, the knowledge of the mysteries is withheld. This is evidently a dispensation analogous to that according to which, as Christ declared, "Many are called, but few are chosen" (Matt. xxii. 14). It is also in accordance with views expressed in a previous part of this Essay respecting the distinction between "the elect" and the rest of mankind.

It is further to be considered that the Lord promised the apostles that after his departure from them, "the Holy Spirit would teach them all things, and bring all things to their remembrance which he had said to them" (John xiv. 26), and it may be assumed that after the Day of Pentecost this promise was fulfilled, and that they were then enlightened to discern the spiritual meaning of his doctrine. In this way it may be accounted for that while Christian doctrine rests fundamentally on the words and deeds of Christ as recorded in the Gospels, it is taught in the Acts of the Apostles and the apostolical Epistles in terms of a more abstract character, which, in fact, may be regarded as unfolding the spiritual import of the teaching, the life, and the death of Jesus Christ. The apostle Paul, although he was not one of the originally selected apostles, had special grace and power given him for understanding fully and teaching the doctrine of Christ. Now, this apostle, so gifted with understanding and knowledge, writes in his Epistle to the Romans: "By the obedience of one shall the many be made righteous" (v. 19); the context evidently showing that the "one" is Jesus Christ, and that "the many" are *all* the sinful sons of Adam. I have already adverted to this text (p. 19), and called attention to the significance of the future tense, "shall be made righteous." According to our argument, when they have been made righteous, they are *saved.* Hence, quite consistently with this passage in the Epistle to the Romans, St. Paul has said in his first Epistle to Timothy (iv. 10), "We trust in the living God, who is the Saviour of all men, especially of those that believe." If this sentence had not contained the last clause, there might have been some excuse for questioning whether St. Paul preached the doctrine of the eventual salvation of all men; but inasmuch as he adds, "especially of those that believe," it is as clear as words can make anything clear, that he taught that all are saved in the sense in which he taught that those who believe are saved. The reason for making the distinction expressed by the word "especially" is, I think, sufficiently apparent from the doctrine, previously maintained in this Essay (pp. 88-40), that the elect righteous are raised up first, and partake already of salvation, honour, and glory, during a certain interval preceding the resurrection of the rest of mankind.

Now, since all that are saved, as being at rest and in felicity, are free from sin and evil, this teaching of St. Paul is directly opposed to the doctrine of the perpetuity of evil which is usually inferred (see p. 71) from the saying of our Lord in Matt. xxv. 46. Thus apparently there is irreconcilable contradiction between the teaching of Christ and the teaching of St. Paul on a most momentous subject. Since, however, the same spirit of wisdom was in the apostle as in his Lord, it is not possible that there can really be such contradiction; and because, consequently, the seeming contradiction must be attributable to our defect of knowledge, or inability, to interpret rightly the allegorical teaching of Christ, we might do well, although no solution of the difficulty should be at hand, to accept this gospel of salvation, in the confidence that, as being declared by St. Paul in plain terms, it must be true Christian doctrine.

I am not, however, prepared to grant that the solution of the above-mentioned difficulty is not discoverable; and accordingly I make bold to indicate a line of argument by which, as it seems to me, a solution is attainable. The first step in this argument is to admit the reality of that analogy between God's natural creation and His spiritual creation which has already been taken into consideration (see p. 14), and to infer therefrom that the spiritual creation is actually in progress towards a foreordained perfect consummation. For the purpose of illustrating this view by way of contrast, I may mention that I once heard a sermon in which the preacher, who was regarded in his day as a leader of religious thought, advanced the theory that the word "remedy" expressed the central idea of the divine scheme of salvation. According to this theology, which looks backwards rather than forwards, the prevalence of sin and mortality, and the need of a remedy for the many ills and errors that beset humanity, were contingent on Adam's transgression. It may be granted that this is so far true, that sin and death entered into the world because Adam was not made incapable of sinning. But this theory overlooks the possibility of there being a *final* cause for the actual facts of humanity, and seems to be a substitution of *propter hoc* for *post hoc.* The analogy of the natural creation points to a different, and apparently a juster, view of the divine economy, according to which the reign of sin and death in Adam and all his posterity is a necessary part of a prearranged scheme, now actually in progress, which is destined, by its completion hereafter, to make, not one man only, but a countless multitude, incapable of sinning and meet for immortality. On this point, however, after what has been already said (see p. 57), there is no occasion to say more here. I proceed, therefore, to the next step, which is to indicate certain inferences that may be drawn from the character of progressiveness which pertains at present to the spiritual creation.

It may, in the first place, be asserted that "the law of opposites," referred to in pp. 69 and 70, is a necessary accompaniment of that general law of progression. The author of the Book of Ecclesiasticus, who certainly put on record many wise sayings, has thus stated the law of opposites: "Good is set against evil, and life against death: so is the sinner against the godly. So look upon all the works of the Most High, and there are two and two, one against another" (xxxiii. 14, 15). Now, evidently this duality will cease, and unity be universally established, when, as argued in the preceding paragraph, the predestined consummation is reached, and the purpose of the whole creation, external and spiritual, is fulfilled. This doctrine of the termination of evil appears to have been understood and proclaimed by the writer of the fourth Book of Esdras, in which we meet with the following emphatic declaration: "Take heaven and earth to witness; for I have broken the evil in pieces, and created the good: for I live, saith the Lord" (ii. 14). In the mean while, as being subject to conditions of earth, and time, and space, we are also subject to this law of duality and antagonism, so that we have no knowledge or perception of anything of which we do not also know the *opposite*. For this reason it is not possible to make known the conditions under which men are saved without at the same time stating the conditions under which they are *not* saved. This will account for the *oppositeness* and *parallelism* of the statements in Matt. xxv. 46, concerning the consequences to the wicked and the righteous of their respective deeds, as well as for many statements of like character in other parts of Scripture. But this does not explain why the punishment of the wicked is said to be "eternal." Relatively to this question I submit the following considerations.

Recurring once more to the position, that the existing order of things is part of a progressive scheme, the purpose of which is to create immortal souls, it may, I think, be reasonably assumed that there is nothing in human cognizance or experience, whether it be thought or feeling, word or deed, which is not contributory in some manner to this end. If a mechanist, after planning a machine for a certain purpose, introduced in the execution of it parts which contributed nothing towards effecting that purpose, would not this be considered to be an imperfection? Such imperfection is wholly inadmissible in the workmanship of an omniscient and omnipotent Creator. Accordingly, since, as being conditioned by *time*, we are capable of entertaining the thought that the punishment of the wicked in the world to come may be eternal, many, in fact, having professed their belief that so it will be, we must conclude, on the above principle, that even this thought is contributory towards the eventual bringing in of immortality. But it will be asked, in what way? To this question we may give the general answer, that as such thought is operative on human action, and implies the existence of *time*, it must be reckoned as part of the total of human thought and experience conditioned by time, which was ordained from the beginning to be the means, whether in this age or in the age to come (*aiôn ho mellôn*), of forming spirits for immortality. Then, again, we have reason from Scripture to infer that the immortal spirit is in effect "spiritual *body*" (I Cor. xv. 44), composed of functional parts or qualities constituting it such a whole that it is adapted for communion with other spirit; in which case the *temporal* processes of creation above mentioned might be supposed to be designed to give to immortal spirit a character appropriate to its destiny. And we may, at least, be certain that Jesus Christ knew what was required for accomplishing his Father's purpose of creating spirits which, while retaining *individuality* and *will*, would be incapable of sinning, and that in his wisdom he employed such manner of teaching as would either now or hereafter conduct to that end.

I take occasion to observe here, parenthetically, that whereas, according to the above argument, the word "eternal" (from *Œetas*) is applicable to punishment because we can think of eternal punishment by thinking of time, the word "endless" is not in the same manner applicable, simply because it does not explicitly indicate relation to *time*. The Greek equivalent of the English word "everlasting," and of the Latin word "*sempiternus*," namely *aidios* from *aei*, is used in Rom. i. 20, and in Jude 6, in the sense of *aiônios*, and, as involving like the latter the conception of time, is similarly applicable to future punishment. But besides "*eternal* life," we have in Scripture "*indissoluble* life" (*xôn akatalytos*, Heb. vii. 16), the remarkable epithet *akatalytos* not being etymologically expressive of time, and therefore not wrongly, although not strictly, translated by "endless" in the Authorized Version. No such epithet is applied in Scripture to "punishment" or "torment." (See more on this question in an Appendix to the Essay.)

Reasoning analogous to that employed above relative to the assertion in Matt. xxv. 46, that the wicked "go away into eternal punishment," is applicable to other declarations of like tenor in various portions of Scripture. One of these, recorded in Matt. xxvi. 24 as having been spoken by the Lord to the "*twelve*," demands special notice. Translated literally according to the tenses of the Greek, this passage is, "Woe to that man through whom the Son of man has been betrayed! good was it for him, if that man was not born." The translation in the Authorized Version, "it had been good for that man if he had not been born," may be taken to convey, regard being had to difference of idiom, the true sense of the original. Exactly the same passage occurs in Mark xiv. 21, where our translators have given, "good were it for that man if he had never been born." Although this translation, as containing the word "never," deviates still more than the other from the literal rendering, it may be justified on the principle that the declaration, in whatever form it be made, is one in which *time* enters as a necessary element, whereby alone it is within the reach of thought. Accordingly, this saying of our Lord, regarded as having relation to experience in the world to come, is in the same category as his assertion of the eternity of future punishment, and would appear, by applying the argument already expounded (p. 80) with respect to that doctrine, to be in like manner contributory towards generating in the spirit of man an incapability of sinning. It is farther to be taken into account that these words were addressed by the Lord to his *apostles*—to the elect of the elect—with particular reference to the sin of *betraying* the Son of man, which was exemplified by the outward act of Judas, who also by his self-destruction exhibited the damnatory power of the inward consciousness of such guilt. The exceeding sinfulness of such apostasy as that which Judas, chosen to be an apostle, was guilty of, may be assigned as the reason that it was denounced by our Lord in terms which do not appear to have been applied to any other kind of "transgression" (compare Acts i. 17, 25).

In Heb. x. 26, 27, we are taught that "if we sin wilfully after that we have received the knowledge of the truth, there remaineth no more sacrifice for sins, but a certain looking for of judgment and fiery indignation, which shall devour the adversaries." This is apostasy not of the same degree and character as that of a chosen apostle, but still is such that "the called" are not exempt from falling into it, as is clearly implied by the tenor of this passage. To those who thus fall and do not repent, is reserved "the fiery indignation" (*pyros zylos*), which is destined hereafter to devour the adversaries. It may be presumed that the adversaries thus specially referred to are those of whom it is said in Rev. xx. 9, that having been deceived by Satan, after their resurrection at the end of the thousand years, and gathered together in warfare against the beloved city, they were *devoured by fire* from God out of heaven. Accordingly their destruction is identical with the second death.

2 Peter ii. 20, 21, is a passage of like import to that just considered. It is therein asserted of those who are overcome by the pollutions of the world after having escaped them through the knowledge of the Lord and Saviour Jesus Christ, that "it had been better for them not to have known the way of righteousness, than, after they have known it, to turn from the holy commandment delivered to them." This may be taken to signify that the punishment in the day of judgment consequent upon sin and error arising out of ignorance, will be "more tolerable" than that which will be inflicted on those who have knowingly apostatized from the way of truth.

What is said in Matt. xviii. 6, "Whoso shall offend one of these little ones that believe in me, it were better for him that a millstone were hanged about his neck, and that he were drowned in the depth of the sea," may be accounted for on the principle that any form of death of which the body is susceptible in this world is rather to be endured, and less to be feared, than the punishment which, through the judgment in the world to come, awaits the enemies of Christ who put a stumbling-block in the way of them that humble themselves as little children and believe on him.

Analogous principles may be applied to account for the declarations made in Scripture respecting blasphemy against the Holy Spirit. In St. Matt. xii. 31, 82, it is recorded that our Lord said, "All sin and blasphemy shall be forgiven to men, but the blasphemy of the Spirit shall not be forgiven to men. And whoever speaketh a word against the Son of man, it shall be forgiven him; but whoever speaketh against the Holy Spirit, it shall not be forgiven him, neither in this world, nor in the world to come." The same doctrine is thus expressed in St. Mark iii. 28, 29: "Verily I say to you, all sins shall be forgiven to the sons of men, and all blasphemies whatever wherewith they may blaspheme. But whoever shall blaspheme against the Holy Ghost hath never forgiveness," but is subject to the judgment in the future *aiôn* (*enochos estin aiôniou kriseôs*). From the latter evangelist we also learn that our Lord spoke these words because the scribes from Jerusalem had said, "He hath an unclean spirit." It is particularly to be noticed that both passages declare in the fullest manner that all manner of sin and blasphemy shall be forgiven to men, at the same time that they pronounce that blasphemy (not sin, *amartia*) against the Holy Ghost is not forgiven. To account for this apparent contradiction, it must be remembered that the forgiveness, or *remission* (*aphesis*) of sin, necessarily implies antecedence of law and transgression of the law; and whereas St. Paul teaches that "the law entered that transgression might abound" (Rom. v. 20), it is quite consistent with this doctrine to find that in the gospel of Christ provision is made for the remission of all sin and blasphemy. Now, such remission consists in "repentance towards God and faith towards our Lord Jesus Christ" (Acts xx. 21); and therefore, when the gift of righteousness (i.e. the grace of Christ) is received, the believer begins to partake of a spirit such as that which was "without measure" in Christ. This is essentially a *holy* spirit, the antecedent of which in Jesus Christ was perfect righteousness. Therefore the scribes blasphemed when they said of Christ, "He hath an unclean spirit," it not being possible that a perfectly righteous body can be the vessel of an unclean spirit.

But it is possible that the faithful, after receiving the grace of Christ and fellowship of the Spirit, may by unrighteous conduct "grieve the Holy Spirit" (Eph. iv. 80), and even by persistence in sin defile the gift of the Spirit which had been imparted to them. In the foregoing passage from St. Matthew xii., it is said that there is forgiveness for one who "speaketh against the Son of man," which expression may signify, generally, wilful and overt opposition to "the law of Christ" (Gal. vi. 2); but that there is no forgiveness for one who *speaks* against the Holy Spirit, i.e. one who by wilful and *overt* conduct does violence to the sanctifying influence of the Holy Spirit which he has already partaken of. Of such an one it is written in Heb. x. 29, "he hath trodden underfoot the Son of God, and hath counted the blood of the covenant wherewith he was sanctified an unholy thing, and hath done despite to the Spirit of grace." But not every sin committed after faith and the baptism of repentance has this effect. The apostle John tells us that although all unrighteousness (*adikia*, transgression of the strict law of Christ) is sin, there is sin of a believing brother which is not unto death, and may be repented of in this world; and there is sin unto death, respecting which prayer for repentance would be unavailing (I Epist. v. 16, 17). This is "the blasphemy of the Spirit," which is not forgiven in this world, because forgiveness implies repentance; neither is it forgiven in the world to come, because beyond the grave there is no repentance. What remains for such sinners is the "Œonian judgment" (see p. 69) mentioned in St. Mark iii. 29, and "the sorer punishment" spoken of in Heb. x. 29, which is the same as the condemnation to the second death consequent upon that judgment. (I take occasion to remark that in Mark iii. 29, instead of *kriseôs*, some early manuscripts have *amaritêmatos*, which, as far as I can see, does not admit of being interpreted consistently with the context and the usage of *enochos*.)

There is still another passage—Mark ix. 42-50—which, on account of its peculiar significance, it is necessary to discuss with reference to the Scriptural argument for immortality. It will suffice for conducting the discussion to cite *vv.* 43 and 44, the literal translation of which is as follows:—"If thy hand cause thee to offend, cut it off: it is well for thee to enter into life maimed, rather than having two hands to go into geenna, into the unquenchable fire, where their worm dieth not, and the fire is not quenched." The concluding part of this text is evidently derived from Isaiah lxvi. 24, where the prophet reveals that the Lord has said respecting the worshippers, consisting of "all flesh," that shall come before him when "the new heavens and the new earth" are established, that "they shall go forth and look upon the carcases of the men that have transgressed against me: for their worm shall not die, neither shall their fire be quenched: and they shall be an abhorring unto all flesh." This passage has so important a bearing on the sense of that quoted above from St. Mark, that we must by all means endeavour to find out its interpretation. Respecting Biblical Interpretation, Burnet in one of his treatises has enunciated two principles, which cannot but be assented to: first, that besides the portions of Scripture which have a literal or historical meaning, there are others which must be taken allegorically; and, secondly, that an allegorical meaning, is to be admitted when the literal sense involves an absurdity, or contradiction to the nature of things.[2] The right application of

---

[2] The treatise referred to is entitled "De Faturâ, Bestauratione," and the passage cited is very near the end of it. This treatise is an appendix to another, the title of which is "De Statu Mortuorum et Resurgentium."

these principles may be said to constitute a large portion of the science of Scripture. But in applying them it is often difficult to decide, respecting a particular passage, whether it is to be taken literally or allegorically; and again, after deciding that the passage must be allegorical, there is generally the still greater difficulty of discovering what the true sense is. In illustration of the second of the above principles Burnet cites, apart from the context, *vermem nunquam moriturum*, and admits that these words have an allegorical signification. This plainly follows from the single consideration that the worm (*skôlêx*) here spoken of is literally that which is seen to feed on dead bodies, and to say of it that it does not die is contradictory to experience. When, however, the same author goes on to give as the allegorical sense nothing more definite than "*extremam miseriam*," it may well be asked, By what kind of induction has this conclusion been reached? The feeble worm which feeds on mortal remains presents to our sight nothing capable of causing pain or misery. Rather it may, I think, be asserted that Scripture here adverts to this natural fact for the purpose of indicating by a distinct and visible emblem that there is a living principle which destroys mortality, and which for that reason alone is not itself subject to death. If we be guided solely by what *we see with our eyes*, this appears to be the only allegorical sense that can be attributed to the first clause of Mark ix. 44.[3] We have next to inquire as to the interpretation of the other clause, and what is the mutual relation between the two clauses.

Although the worm which devours dead bodies is not emblematic of anything that causes pain, the case is quite otherwise with respect to the emblematic meaning of *fire*. It is evident that fire which is "unquenchable" is not natural fire, and consequently may be taken to be, as has already been assumed, the devouring fire of judgment and of condemnation consequent

---

[3] So far this explanation of Mark ix. 44 is the same as that which I have given in a letter to the editor of the *Clerical Journal*, which is inserted in the number for June 5, 1862 (p. 526).

upon violation of the law of righteousness (see p. 88). The destruction of the impenitent unrighteous by the operation of this law (which is their second death), is attended with pain and woe such as will not have been before, nor will be after. It was inferred (p. 84) from our Lord's teaching in Matt. xviii. 6, that any form of *death* of which the body is susceptible in this world is rather to be endured than falling under condemnation in the world to come. In Mark ix. 42-48, we are taught that any form of bodily *pain*, as that of losing a hand, a foot, or an eye, is to be preferred to entering with the body whole into the "*geenna* of fire." This is, in fact, at once the greatest and the *last* of human suffering and tribulation. For it should be noticed that at the end of this very passage (v. 49) it is said that "every one shall be salted [made 'good,' *v.* 50] with fire," signifying the effect finally produced by the unquenchable fire. And with this agrees the emblem of the worm that "dieth not," taken as indicating that the final effect of the torment of the judgment is to swallow up death, and to bring in, by establishing the reign of righteousness, life and immortality. The signification of one emblem must be taken in conjunction with that of the other.

Moreover, by giving particular attention to the context of Isa. lxvi. 24, it will be seen that what is there revealed is quite in accordance with the above interpretation. For, first, in *v.* 16 we have, "By fire and by his sword [the sword of the Word of God spoken of in Rev. xix. 15] will the Lord plead with all flesh," that is, in the judgment which has been appointed for the trial and tribulation of all men. Then, by taking into account what is said in *vv.* 22 and 23, we may gather that "all flesh," having become denizens of "the new heavens and the new earth" in which, as St. Peter declares (2 Epist. iii. 13), righteousness dwells, "come to worship the Lord." Of *these worshippers*, consisting of "all flesh," it is affirmed that "they shall go forth and look upon the carcases of the transgressors," which, on account of the ill savour coming up from them, will be "an abhorring to all flesh" (compare Isa. xxxiv. 3). Thus there is here represented, but by a different figure, the same truth as that which has already been deduced from the ascending up for ever and ever of the brimstone smoke of torment (see pp. 61 and 65); namely, that the subjecting of all the deeds and secrets of the present life to the scrutiny of judgment, and the consequent condemnation of all the unredeemed to the pains of a second death, will have the effect of making sin against a "faithful Creator" to be seen and felt to be so hateful and abominable a thing, that such sin will cease to be possible, notwithstanding that all men will retain individuality and volition. For all will thus at length be made new creatures incapable of sinning. This remark may serve to introduce the final stage of the general argument, which I now proceed to enter upon.

I have been endeavouring to show that the symbolic assertions in Rev. xx. respecting "the lake of fire" and its "burning with brimstone," the casting therein of the devil, the beast, and the false prophet, and their being tormented "day and night for ever and ever," the judgment of all the dead, small and great, according to their recorded deeds, "the second death," and the casting into the lake of fire of "any one not found written in the book of life," do not necessitate, as is commonly thought, the conclusion that evil, which had a beginning, fulfils no purpose and has no ending. As to this question the seer gives, in Rev. xxi. 1-4, the following explicit revelation: "And I saw a new heaven and a new earth: for the first heaven and the first earth passed away; and there is no more sea. And I saw the holy city, new Jerusalem, coming down out of heaven from God, prepared as a bride adorned for her husband. And I heard a great voice from the throne, saying, Behold, the tabernacle of God is with men, and He will dwell with them, and they shall be His people, and God Himself will be with them, their God. And God will wipe away every tear from their eyes; and death shall be no more, neither sorrow nor crying, neither shall there be any more pain: for the first things passed away." Now, it seems hardly possible that the announcement of the termination of evil could be made in terms more direct and more intelligible than these. Hence, according to acknowledged principles of Biblical interpretation, we must not attribute to the above-mentioned symbolic and less intelligible passages any meaning inconsistent with that announcement. The arguments I have adduced respecting the interpretation of the figurative statements contained in the latter half of chap. xx. are directed to showing that these figures do, in fact, admit of meanings consistent with the gospel revelations given in chap. xxi. 1-4. It is of so much importance, as regards the Scriptural doctrine of immortality, to establish this point, that I propose now to supplement the former arguments by additional considerations.

In the Book of Daniel (xii. 6, 7) we read of "a man clothed in linen, who was upon the water of a river, and held up his right hand and his left hand unto heaven, and sware by Him that liveth for ever," that at the end of an appointed time a certain purpose would be accomplished, and "all these things be finished." This refers, as the context shows, to "the time of the end" of the present age (*aiôn*). The announcement made in this manner by the man clothed in linen indicates that he is the precursor of the angel of whom, in *vv.* 1, 2, 5, 6, 7 of Rev. x., the apostle John relates as follows: "I saw a mighty angel come down from heaven, clothed with a cloud, and a rainbow upon his head, and his face as the sun, and his feet as pillars of fire; and, having in his hand a little book open, he set his right foot upon the sea, and his left foot upon the earth.... and lifted up his hand to heaven, and sware by Him that liveth for ever and ever, who created heaven and the things therein, and the earth and the things therein, and the sea and the things therein, that time shall be no more; but in the days of the voice of the seventh angel, in the time when he is about to sound his trumpet, also [*kai,* merely indicating the apodosis] the mystery of God is finished (*etelesthê,* aor. ind.), according to the gospel He made known to His servants the prophets." The soundings of the seven trumpets are significant of progressive steps in the general judgment; the days pertaining to the voice of the seventh angel are those immediately preceding the actual sounding of his trumpet, which announces the completion (as indicated by the number seven) of the mystery of God's creation in time, and marks the end of the age (*ho aiôn ho mellôn*) following upon the conclusion of the present age. When all that pertains to this final interval "is finished," there is no more succession of events whereby time is cognizable, and therefore time is no more. The might, and glorious investiture, and majestic attitude of the angel who proclaims this truth, conspire to point out its great significance. The little book in his hand is the word of prophecy by which we learn these mysteries.

It is, no doubt, beyond the limit of our thoughts, conditioned as we are by time, to conceive of a state of things in which time is no more. Apparently for this reason commentators have proposed to translate, *chronos ouk estai eti,* "the time shall not be yet," or "time shall no more intervene." The former of these translations is excluded by the usage of *ouk eti* in the analogous affirmations in Rev. xxi. 1, 4, and the other, which is an arbitrary comment rather than a translation, is for the same reason excluded. (I have preferred *ouk estai eti* to *ouketi estai,* because the words occur in the former order in each of the three instances in Rev. xxi.) There can be no question as to the philological correctness of the translation, "time shall be no more." The unwillingness to admit it appears to have arisen solely from a fixed persuasion, gratuitously and very generally entertained, that time has a *necessary* existence, and therefore cannot come to an end. Some have affirmed that when time ends, eternity begins; which is a self-contradictory dogma, because eternity (from *Œtas*) is essentially time. The teaching of Scripture on this point is directly opposed to these views; for the apostle Peter tells those for whose sake he wrote his second Epistle, to bear in mind "this one thing, that one day is with the Lord as a thousand years, and a thousand years as one day" (2 Epist. iii. 8). This is equivalent to saying that time is not an independent entity, but that both its existence and its quality are determined by the *will* of the Creator of all things. It is in virtue of our being made in His image, and partaking intellectually of the divine nature, that we are capable *in thought* of giving indefinite and arbitrary extension to time, whether it be past time or time to come. This faculty, as I have already argued in p. 80, is to be placed in the category of the different conditions, whether depending on experience of the course of time, or on affections of our bodily and mental constitutions, under which the spirit of man is formed for immortality. All such conditions are determined by the purpose for which they are imposed, and when that purpose is fulfilled in the perfection of humanity the conditions come to an end. It is thus that the being conditioned by time eventually ceases.

It will be proper here to meet an objection to the doctrine that time will have an end which might be drawn from the expression, *eis tous aiônas tôn aiônôn*, which frequently occurs in Scripture, and seems to be indicative of an unlimited succession of ages. So far as time is under human cognizance, and has relation to human experience, Scripture speaks in express terms of only *two* ages—the present one, which lasts to the end of the *generations* of men in the existing order of things; and the age to come, which embraces the course of the judgment of all who lived in the first age, and terminates with the second death of those who had no part in the first resurrection. When it is said of the Creator of heaven and earth, that He is "from everlasting to everlasting" (*apo tou aiônos meôs tou aiônos su ei*, Ps. xc. 2), and that "He liveth for ever and ever" (*ho zôn eis tous aiônas tôn aiônôn*, Rev. x. 6), the word *aiôn* is not used to signify, as in the instances of the two "ages" just mentioned, an interval having beginning and ending, but is to be taken in an abstract sense, derived from our ordinary perception of the existence and quality of time, and from the faculty which, as said before, we possess of thinking of time as indefinitely extended. The first of the cited passages affirms what in these days we should express by saying that God is necessarily and essentially self-existent, and the other, what we mean by saying that He is necessarily and essentially a *living* God. But Scripture uses no such terms as these, because it is written on the principle of employing in an abstract sense only such terms as are rendered intelligible by personal sensation and observation, and by experience drawn under actual conditions from the outer world. It is thus that the word "age" acquired its primary meaning, before it was susceptible of the abstract application just mentioned.

There is also to be said, as a reason for accepting this doctrine respecting our relation to time, that Scripture teaches analogous doctrine respecting our relation to *space*. When our Lord astonished his disciples by saying that the passage of a camel through the eye of a needle is not an impossibility, he explained that "this is impossible with men, but not with God; for with God all things are possible" (Mark x. 25-27). By this saying he asserted that space, and the mutual relations of body and space, are such as they are by the will and power of God, and by the same power might be changed. Considering, therefore, that "the new heavens and the new earth" constitute a "new creation," it is quite in accordance with the above inference from our Lord's words to find it said of "the new Jerusalem, the holy city," that "the length, and the breadth, and the height of it are equal" (Rev. xxi. 16). For a city to be such as to conform to this description, it is plain that material substance and space must be related to each other in an entirely new manner, unrecognizable by present experience. The apostle Paul adverts to the eventual status of the spirit of man with respect to time and space where he says, "I am persuaded that neither death, nor life, nor angels, nor principalities, nor things present, nor things to come, nor powers, nor height, nor depth, nor any other creation, will be able to separate us from the love of God, which is in Christ Jesus our Lord" (Rom. viii. 38, 39). (In this sentence the recognized passage of time, the powers [*dynameis*] of nature, and the measurable qualities of space, seem all to be regarded as things *created*.) Also corresponding to the change in the external creation it is revealed that there will be a change of the outward man, the natural body giving place to the "spiritual body." It would appear, therefore, from the whole of the foregoing argument that our spirits, after being bound by earthly and temporal conditions, undergo complete transformation, being conjoined with bodily essence related in a new manner to *space*, and being also released from the condition of *time*. But although this mode of existence may be a necessary condition of the immortal state, especially as such state embraces associated members, it is not the sole, nor the principal, condition of immortality, as the remainder of the argument will show.

It has already been noticed that St. Peter characterizes "the new heavens and the new earth" by saying that "righteousness dwells therein." This is as much as to say that it is a perfect *social* state, whose end is at once the glory of God and the happiness of man. The words of the apostle (2 Epist. iii. 13) signify that the new creation, by satisfying this condition, is the fulfilment of an antecedent promise. Now, the argument of this Essay is in entire agreement with this doctrine, inasmuch as it was from the first assumed (p. 9) that immortality cannot consist with any other than a state of righteousness, and then (pp. 19 and 20) it was argued that after Adam's transgression a *promise* was made that himself and his race would eventually be exempt from the power of Satan and attain to immortality. The passage Rev. xxi. 1-4, quoted in p. 92, seems to certify the complete fulfilment of this promise and to indicate the manner of its fulfilment. But there are other passages in this concluding portion of the Apocalypse, which might be thought to bear a contrary signification, to which, therefore, our attention must now be directed.

In xxi. 8 we have, "But the fearful, and unbelieving, and the abominable, and murderers, and fornicators, and sorcerers, and idolaters, and all lies, shall have their part in the lake which burneth with fire and brimstone: which is the second death." If we give to this symbolism, as consistency requires, an interpretation analogous to that applied to Rev. xx. 10, we shall conclude that sinners of all classes will eventually have no cognizable existence, transgression being brought to an end by the effect of the general judgment and the pains of the second death. This may explain why it is added, "which is the second death." It is worthy of remark that "all lies" are said to have their part in "the lake" although the casting of lies into a lake is objectively an impossibility. But this variation of the designation ("lies" being put for "liars") may be intended to signify generally that all transgression disappears, because transgressors cease to be cognizable *as transgressors.*

There is another thing to be noticed respecting the same passage: it contains no such clause as, "They shall be tormented day and night to the ages of ages," which occurs at the end of Rev. xx. 10. This omission may be accounted for on the principle stated in p. 96, according to which expressions involving time are not applicable to the condition of things in the new creation, in which time exists no more.

I take the occasion to remark here that the above-cited clause appears to be the only passage in the Apocalypse which asserts the perpetuity of *personal* experience of torment, as distinct from the perpetuity of its effect; also that the personal subject of the verb *basanisthêsontia,* according to grammatical rules, would be the devil, the beast, and the false prophet, each of which is represented as personal, and endowed with volition and power. But these, as I have maintained in p. 61, are the powers which, according to the law of opposites, are antagonist to God the Father, the Holy Ghost, and the Son of God; and the assertion that they are tormented for ever and ever may be taken to mean, according to the principle of interpretation explained in p. 97, that they exist *necessarily,* but only as they exist, when subdued, in the contempt and hatred in which they are held by those who have felt their power and have overcome it, this spiritual effect being a condition of immortality. (See end of p. 61.)

It remains to speak of one other subject connected with the revelations made in the Apocalypse, which, understood as it respects our argument, is of very great moment, inasmuch as it has relation to the means by which the spirit of man is endowed with immortality. The Son of God is named in the Apocalypse "The Word of God" (xix. 18), "King of kings and Lord of lords" (xvii. 14, and xix. 16), "the root and the offspring of David, the bright and morning star" (xxii. 16), and by other titles expressive of honour and dignity; but no name occurs so frequently, and in such various applications, as "the Lamb." What, it may be asked, is the reason for this? In order to answer this question let us take into consideration some instances, specially significant, in which this name occurs. From what is recorded in chap. v. 6-13 as having been seen in vision by the apostle, we are instructed as follows respecting the character and office of the Lamb: "In the midst of the throne [the seat of the Lord God Almighty] and of the four living beings, and in the midst of the elders, stood a Lamb as it had been slain, having seven horns [emblematic of perfect power] and seven eyes [perfection of wisdom], which are the seven Spirits of God sent forth into all the earth." And he came and took out of the right hand of Him who sat upon the throne a book "sealed with seven seals." "And when he had taken the book, the four living beings and four and twenty elders fell down before the Lamb.... And they sung a new song, saying, Thou art worthy to take the book, and to open the seals thereof; for thou wast slain." Then "an innumerable company of angels" (Heb. xii. 22) was heard to say with a loud voice, "Worthy is the Lamb that was slain to receive power, and riches, and wisdom, and strength, and honour, and glory, and blessing. And every created thing which is in heaven, and on the earth, and under the earth, and such as are in the sea, and all things in them, were heard to say, Blessing, and honour, and glory, and power be unto Him that sitteth upon the throne, and unto the Lamb for ever and ever."

Then follows in chap. vi. the opening of the seven seals, which, from the descriptions given at the successive openings, appear to symbolize the various kinds of human experience, both good and evil, which mark the course of events in the present world, all centering in the work of redemption by the sacrifice of the Son of God; on which account the Lamb *slain* can alone open the seven seals and disclose their meaning. At the end of what is said relative to the sixth seal mention is made of "the great day of the wrath of the Lamb," which, because by reason of the sins of men he was so unjustly slain, is ordained to be seen and felt by the whole world after the termination of the present age (see Rev. i. 7). The expectation of that wrath, although none can escape it, all but very few in the present day are unwilling, through terror or unbelief, to entertain. The state of terror of all classes at the signs of the approach of that day appears to be described at the end of the chapter. (See vi. *vv.* 15-17.)

Next, in chap. vii., comes the sealing of all the elect, represented symbolically by the sealing of twelve thousand of each of the twelve tribes of Israel, the number twelve specially signifying election. Then in *vv.* 9-17 is recorded a most wonderful vision. The seer says, "After this I beheld, and, lo, a great multitude, whom no man could number, of all nations, and tribes, and peoples, and tongues, standing before the throne and before the Lamb, clothed with white robes, and palms in their hands: and they cry with a loud voice, saying, Salvation to our God who sitteth upon the throne, and to the Lamb." This multitude whom no man can number, the number of whom is elsewhere said to be as "the sand of the sea," must embrace all that are not of the number of the elected and sealed one hundred and forty-four thousand, and their ascription here of praise to God for salvation accords with the teaching of St. Paul, that "God is the Saviour of all men, especially of those that believe." This is made still plainer by what is said respecting this multitude clothed in white robes in *vv.* 14-17. The seer is told by one of the elders that "These are they who come out of the great tribulation, and washed their robes, and made them white in the blood of the Lamb. Therefore are they before the throne of God, and serve Him day and night in His temple; and He that sitteth on the throne shall dwell among them. And they shall hunger no more, neither thirst any more; neither shall the sun light on them, nor any heat. For the Lamb who is in the midst of the throne will feed them, and will lead them to fountains of waters of life; and God will wipe away all tears from their eyes." It is evident that the revelation here made is *proleptical,* describing a state of things identical with that which in Rev. xxi. 3, 4 (before quoted in p. 93), is said to pertain to the new heavens and the new earth. The explanation that may be given of this anticipation of the subsequent revelation is referable to a principle which governs much that is contained in Scripture, although it has been generally overlooked—the principle, namely, of following sometimes an order determined by *relativity*, although it sets aside order as to time. This, however, is not done except for some purpose. In the present instance, the effect of declaring the salvation of all men in immediate sequence to the sealing of the elect for salvation, is to indicate that the general scheme whereby all eventually partake of salvation consists of related and progressive parts to be unfolded by course of time.

The name of "the Lamb" is also given to our Lord in various other passages, which, with the view of contributing to the general argument, I proceed now to cite and make some remarks upon. The accuser of the brethren (Satan) is overcome by those who loved not their lives unto death, "on account of the *blood* of the Lamb" (xii. 10, 11). The beast will be worshipped by all dwellers upon earth "whose names are not written in the book of life of the Lamb *slain* from the foundation of the world" (xiii. 8). "A Lamb stood on the mount Sion, and with him an hundred forty and four thousand, having his Father's name written on their foreheads.... These are they who follow the Lamb wheresoever he goeth. These were purchased from among men, the firstfruits to God and to the Lamb" (xiv. 1, 4). The worshippers of the beast "shall be tormented with fire and brimstone in the presence of the holy angels and in the presence of the Lamb" (xiv. 10). Those who have gotten the victory over the beast "sing the song of Moses the servant of God, and the song of the Lamb, saying, Great and marvellous are thy works, Lord God Almighty; just and true are thy ways, thou King of the nations. Who shall not fear thee, O Lord, and glorify thy name? for thou only art holy: for all nations shall come and worship before thee, because thy judgments are made manifest" (xv. 2-4). The law given by Moses, and the gospel of Jesus Christ, constitute together a great and wonderful Œconomy, redounding to the praise and glory of God, and to the salvation of man. Kings of the earth "shall make war with the Lamb, and the Lamb shall overcome them, because he is Lord of lords and King of kings, and they that are with him are called, and elect, and faithful" (xvii. 14).

The marriage of the Lamb and his bride—that is, the union of Christ with the whole assembly of the redeemed—does not take place till "the wife has made herself ready," till she has arrayed herself in the fine linen, clean and white, which it was given her to put on, the fine linen being "the righteousness of saints" (xix. 7, 8). This doctrine accords well with the view taken throughout this Essay, namely, that righteousness (the "unspeakable gift," 2 Cor. ix. 15) is necessary as an antecedent condition of salvation, and therefore of immortality. It is further to be noticed that this union between the Lamb and the bride is not perfected while time lasts, requiring the condition of a new creation. For it was not till the first heaven and the first earth passed away that John "saw the holy city, new Jerusalem, coming down from God out of heaven, prepared as a bride adorned for her husband" (xxi. 2), and that "the Lamb's wife" was shown to him by "one of the seven angels that had the seven vials full of the last seven plagues" (xxi. 9). The performance of this office by an angel who in the antecedent judgment had been a minister of wrath and punishment, may be taken to be significant of the *means* by which the glorious consummation is brought about.

Finally, we have in the following concluding portions of apocalyptic prophecy a description of what may be said to constitute the joy of the marriage supper, namely, the perfection through righteousness, not only of the union between Christ and the elect Church, but also of that between God and all peoples. Speaking of "the holy city Jerusalem," John says, "I saw no temple therein; for the Lord God Almighty and the Lamb are the temple of it. And the city hath no need of the sun, neither of the moon, to shine on it; for the glory of God gave light to it, and the Lamb is the lamp thereof. And the nations shall walk by the light of it, and the kings of the earth bring their glory into it. And the gates of it shall not be shut by day, for there will not be night there. And they shall bring the glory and honour of the nations into it. And there shall not enter into it anything unclean, and that worketh abomination and lying, but only they that are written in the Lamb's book of life" (xxi. 22-27). The seer goes on to say, "And he showed me a river of water of life, bright as crystal, coming forth from the throne of God and of the Lamb. In the midst of the street of it and of the river, on the one side and the other [the river being in the middle of the street, and the tree spreading from one side to the other], was the tree of life, producing twelve fruits, and yielding its fruit according to each month; and the leaves of the tree are for the healing of the nations. And there shall be no more curse; and the throne of God and of the Lamb shall be in it, and His servants shall serve Him: and they shall see His face, and His name shall be on their foreheads. And night shall be no more: and they shall have no need of light of a lamp, and light of the sun; because the Lord God will give them light, and they shall reign to the ages of ages" (xxii. 1-5).

The foregoing citations, and indeed the whole tenor of the contents of the Apocalypse, clearly point to the conclusion that what is symbolized by "the Lamb" and "the Lamb slain" runs through all it teaches respecting the course of experience and future destination of the race of man—is "the lamp" that enlightens the whole. Now, I think I may assert that the reason this is so is given by the arguments adduced in this Essay. It has been maintained that on the day that Adam fell into disobedience by the wiles of Satan, his Creator made a promise by covenant that he and his offspring should in the end be freed from the power of Satan and evil, and partake of immortality. The terms of the covenant were that man must pass through toil, and pain, and death, that thereby his spirit might be formed for receiving the gift of an immortal life. Evidence of an intelligent belief of the efficacy of these conditions was given by the faithful of old by their sacrificing clean animals, and surety for the fulfilment of the covenant was given on God's part by a favourable acceptance, either directly or mediately, of this expression of their faith. In process of time the only begotten Son of God, out of sympathy with suffering humanity, and from knowledge of his Father's purpose towards us, satisfied in his own person the very same conditions, and thus at once exemplified and justified the means by which that purpose is accomplished. At the same time he made sure the grounds for belief of the fulfilment of the covenanted promise, first by marvellous works before he suffered, which showed that he had command over all the ills of humanity, and after his death, by resurrection from the grave the third day, which gave proof of the reality of a power that could overcome death. The miracles of Christ are an essential part of the work of his ministry, inasmuch as they were needed to prove that he possessed power greater than that of his adversaries, and consequently that he submitted *voluntarily* to be "led as a *lamb* to the slaughter," and to endure all the pain and indignities of the cross. Out of love towards those whom he vouchsafes to call his brethren, he showed how they must undergo physical suffering and the pains of death in order that their spirits might be formed for an endless life. It was with understanding and belief that the way to life was made sure by fellowship with Christ in suffering, that some of the most favoured of his faithful followers, apostles and apostolic men, willingly suffered after his example.

But pain and death are not in this way efficacious for salvation, unless they be accompanied by a faith which lays hold of the covenant and promise of life made and ratified from the beginning by God, and which looks for the fulfilment in the world to come. Those who, having this faith, do good works are God's elect, who live again at the first resurrection, to die no more. The rest of mankind, although they go through suffering and death, and although their sufferings are not without effect in forming their spirits for immortality (such is the virtue of the sacrifice of the Son of God "for the sins of the whole world"), rise to be judged for their unbelief and unrighteousness, and to be condemned to undergo a second death. The Lamb slain is appointed to execute the judgment and take vengeance on the unrighteous. What better title could there be for his undertaking this "strange work" (Isa. xxviii. 21), than his having so cruelly and unjustly suffered at the hands of sinful men? Yet the portions of Scripture we have had under consideration necessitate the conclusion that the consecration of the way to life through death by the death of the Son of God, which applies to the death of believers, applies also to the second death of unbelievers; so that this death also is followed by life. But here a difficulty presents itself which needs explanation. Although Scripture speaks of a first resurrection and a second death, it makes no mention of a *second resurrection.* This, I think, may be accounted for as follows.

By considering the context, both preceding and following, of the clause, "This is the first resurrection," in Rev. xx. 5, it will be apparent that "resurrection" does not here mean simply returning to life after death, but may be taken to embrace the whole period of the thousand years, together with all that concerns "the happy and the holy" who have part therein. This interpretation is in accordance with the sense in which our Lord speaks of resurrection where he says, "In the resurrection they neither marry nor are given in marriage, but are as the angels, of God in heaven" (Matt. xxii. 30). That "the resurrection" (*hê anastasis*) designates a state or condition of life into which the elect of God are *introduced* by returning to life after death, is still more explicitly signified by the following corresponding passage of St. Luke (xx. 34-36): "The children of this world marry, and are given in marriage; but they who are accounted worthy to obtain that world, and the resurrection from the dead, neither marry nor are given in marriage: neither can they die any more; for they are equal to the angels, and are children of God, being children of the resurrection." Now, it may certainly be inferred from what is said in Rev. xx. 5, that the rest of the dead, who have no part in this first resurrection, return to life at the end of the thousand years. But they return to life to be judged, condemned, and suffer death again. This, therefore, is in no sense a resurrection answering to the description above given of the first resurrection, and accordingly is not called in Scripture the second resurrection. What really corresponds to the holiness and happiness of the first resurrection state is the finally perfected and all-comprehending state called "the new heaven and the new earth," life in which, according to our argument, comes out of the second and last death, and is unconditioned by time. This is the heavenly state which is described in Rev. vii. 11-17, xxi. 2-4, and 10-27. Thus, although this may be regarded as that subsequent resurrection to which "the first resurrection" by its very designation points, it is not called "the second resurrection," because it is not, like the first, limited or conditioned by *time*.

The portion of the Apocalypse which is strictly symbolical and prophetical begins at *v.* 1 of chap. iv. and ends with *v.* 5 of chap. xxii. The first three chapters, including the epistles to the seven Churches, and the verses from chap. xxii. 5 to the end of the book, may be taken to be respectively introduction and conclusion, the contents of which, although strictly related to those of the intermediate symbolical part, are not of a character so exclusively figurative. This circumstance has to be taken into account in proposing interpretations of passages contained in them. Now, there are certain passages in the concluding part which appear to be contradictory to the doctrine of salvation maintained in this Essay, and accordingly, before bringing the argument to a close, I shall endeavour to ascertain the true interpretations of these passages.

The angel who showed John "these things" (xxii. 8) says of himself, "I am the fellow-servant of thee, and of thy brethren the prophets, and of those who keep the words of this book;" and yet this speaker is not distinguished from him who afterwards says (*vv.* 12, 13), "Lo, I come quickly, and my reward is with me, to render to each according as his work is. I am the Alpha and the Omega, the first and the last, the beginning and the end," who, without doubt, is the Lord himself. This may be accounted for by the following considerations. This angel, of whom it is twice asserted that he refused to receive worship proffered to him by the seer (xix. 10, and xxii. 9), is the same that is spoken of in Rev. i. 1, with reference to "the revelation of Jesus Christ, which God gave to him, to shew to his servants things which must shortly come to pass," in these terms: "He [Jesus Christ] by sending

signified it [the revelation] through his angel to his servant John."
In certain passages in the introductory part of the Apocalypse, as
Rev. i. 8, 17-20, and throughout the epistles to the seven
Churches, the Lord speaks in his own person; and this again he
does expressly in some passages in the concluding part, as xxii. 7,
12, 13, 16, 20; and although the speaker in *vv.* 10 and 11 appears
to be the same as the speaker in *v.* 9, who certainly is the angel,
such words as those two verses contain could hardly have been
uttered by any one but the Lord, and, at least, they may be
attributed to him on the principle that what the Lord does
through his ministering angel may be said to be done by himself.
It is as ministering to Jesus Christ that the angel calls himself a
"fellow-servant" of prophets and apostles, and, generally, of those
who keep the words of this revelation. For these reasons in the
following remarks I take *vv.* 10 and 11 as spoken by Jesus Christ.

The words addressed by the speaker to John are (*vv.* 10, 11):
"Seal not the sayings of the prophecy of this book; for the time is
at hand. He who is unrighteous, let him commit injustice still;
and he who is filthy, let him be filthy still; and he who is
righteous, let him do righteousness still; and he who is holy, let
him be holy still. Lo, I come quickly; and my reward is with me,
to render to each as his work is." This passage has been
interpreted as meaning that in the world to come the conditions
of the righteous and the wicked are irrevocably fixed.

I would rather say, having regard to the precise opposition of
the clauses of which it is composed, that the passage declares that
in the end unrighteousness and filthiness are irrevocably separate
from their opposites righteousness and holiness; and to account
for the terms in which this statement is made, it may suffice to
refer to the principle that according to the concrete, or objective,
teaching of the Apocalypse, holiness and filthiness would not be
spoken of abstractedly, that is, apart from holy and *filthy* persons,
and in like manner righteousness and unrighteousness would not
be mentioned apart from their necessary antecedents, *personal*
righteous and unrighteous *deeds.* The expressions "commit

injustice" and "do righteousness," which do not occur in the English version, are exact renderings of the Greek.

Another passage which, as bearing on our argument, requires to be taken into account, is *v.* 15 of the same chapter, which asserts that "without are dogs, and sorcerers, and fornicators, and murderers, and idolaters, and every one that loveth and maketh a lie." This is expressing in concrete language, such as is constantly employed in Scripture, that there is no unrighteousness in the city of God. Such language, being concerned only with *objective* realities, cannot express a *negation,* and, consequently, cannot assert that unrighteousness is *not* within the city. Hence it is not possible, except by means of such terms as those actually employed, to express concretely that the city of God is free from all unrighteousness. By comparing Rev. xxi. 8 with the interpretation here given of Rev. xxii. 15, it will be seen that the exclusion from the city of God of all things sinful and abominable is declared to be effected by "the second death."

I have now completed the argument respecting man's immortality which I proposed to found upon the words of Scripture. I have argued on the hypothesis that for this purpose the Scriptures are trustworthy and sufficient, and I have admitted that we can know nothing for certain concerning our immortality apart from the declared will of "Him who alone hath immortality" (I Tim. vi. 16). Accordingly, Scripture must be consulted in order to learn what God has willed respecting the destiny of man. The principal result of this inquiry is, that by the will of God righteousness and salvation are so inseparably connected that only as being personally righteous can man be saved and partake of immortality. The question, therefore, as to the immortality of all men resolves itself into inquiring whether, and by what means, all men are made righteous. Arguments relating to this inquiry may be said to constitute the whole of this Essay. I am prepared to expect that it will be objected to these arguments that they are *new,* and on this account that the conclusions drawn from them are not *true.* I admit the validity of this inference if the arguments and conclusions are really new, but

I maintain that in so far as they are founded upon, and correctly supported by, Scripture, they cannot be new, because we must not suppose that the Scriptural doctrine of man's salvation was not fully understood before these days—for instance, in the days of primitive Christianity. As the objection on the ground of newness cannot be sustained, the only course left to the objector is to examine the arguments, for the purpose of ascertaining whether they are sound and strictly Scriptural.

I think, however, it is possible that Scriptural doctrine, as taught originally by prophets, apostles, and apostolic men, may have become so obscured and mixed up with human traditions and accretions, that bringing it again to light would appear like promulgating new doctrine. This remark leads me to state on what authorities I have chiefly relied in the composition of this Essay. I may say at once that my views have been determined for the most part by long study of St. Paul's Epistle to the Romans, and the Apocalypse of the Apostle John. I was not, however, able to accept St. Paul's Epistle as it is translated in the Authorized Version, nor could I agree with any commentary upon it that had come before me. For these reasons I published a revised Translation, with Introduction and Notes (Deighton, Bell, & Co., 1871), which may, perhaps, claim consideration, if on no other ground, because it is the production of a mind not unacquainted with classical studies, but trained especially by mathematics and the pursuit of physical science for inquiring respecting the method and laws of divine operation. I have stated in the preface to that work (p. x.) the particular bearing which, as it seemed to me, such studies have on the interpretation of St. Paul's Epistle. Under the influence of the same mental training, I was induced long since to direct my attention towards the interpretation of the Apocalypse, and I purpose shortly, if God be willing, to publish the fruits of my researches. Any reader of this Essay will perceive that it contains much which depends on views which I entertain respecting the general scheme and the symbolism of the Apocalypse.

With respect to the interpretation of symbolical Scripture, I have not abstained from having recourse to books which, although they are not included in the Canon of Scripture, are specially adapted to reveal principles on which the prophetical and symbolical parts of Canonical Scripture may be interpreted. I refer to three books in particular, the fourth Book of Esdras, the Epistle of Barnabas, and the Shepherd of Hermas. There is historic evidence that these books were largely made use of in the days of primitive Christianity. The first has obtained an honourable place in the Articles of the Church of England, owing, no doubt, to the traditional influence which the Church of Rome still had at the time of the Reformation. In the midst of much error and superstition pervading that Church, she faithfully performed the part of keeper of the ancient sacred writings, and to her we are indebted for the preservation for ecclesiastical use of that most instructive book, although at the Council of Trent it was not admitted into the Romish Canon. The other two books above mentioned were long regarded by the Primitive Church as being useful for instruction in doctrine, and of authority little less than that of Scripture; in attestation of which assertion it may be stated that the Codex Sinaiticus contains the whole of the Epistle of Barnabas, and a portion of the Shepherd of Hermas, although no other early Christian writings are in the same manner associated with the Canonical Books.

In drawing inferences from the above sources of information, I have endeavoured to keep closely to the rules of induction which have conducted to such signal discoveries in Natural Philosophy, and to refrain from accepting any inference which the Scriptural data did not justify. The modern advances in physical science, which have shown in what path we must proceed in order to reach a knowledge of God's works, indicate, it may be presumed, that an analogous method is to be pursued in order to gain a knowledge of His word. But it will, perhaps, be said, that if the knowledge of what is revealed in Scripture be obtainable only by means such as those which have been exemplified in this Essay, the considerations that must be entered into are so remote from common apprehension, that but very few can be supposed to be endowed with capacity for understanding them. This, it must be admitted, is actually the case, and, besides, is in conformity with the arbitrament according to which God grants to an elected few gifts and graces which He withholds from the many.

Yet it seems to be the will of God to vouchsafe at certain times and places, and among certain peoples, a more than ordinary measure of knowledge; and perhaps we shall not err in believing that the prophecy in the Book of Daniel, "Many shall run to and fro, and knowledge shall be increased" (xii. 4), is being fulfilled in our time and nation. There is also a remarkable passage in the Apocalypse, which seems to reveal that before "the time of the end" (Dan. xii. 4), the gospel in its most comprehensive sense will be preached among all nations: "And I saw another angel flying in mid-heaven, having the Œonian gospel [i.e. the gospel pertaining to the future age] to preach to those that dwell upon the earth, and to every nation and tribe and tongue and people, saying with a loud voice, Fear God, and give Him glory because the hour of His judgment is come: and worship Him who made the heaven, and the earth, and the sea, and fountains of waters" (Rev. xiv. 6, 7). I cannot forbear noticing the coincidence of the plain meaning of the words of this prophecy with the views advocated in this Essay: first, in respect to calling the gospel "Œonian" and thus asserting its applicability to the future age; next, in its announcement of the gospel in connection with the advent of "the hour of judgment;" and, lastly, in the loud call the angel makes to the dwellers on earth to give glory and worship to the Creator of heaven, earth, sea, and the fountains of waters.

But the dulness of hearers and incapacity to understand the doctrine of Scripture are not the only obstacles those will have to contend against who undertake to preach "the Œonian gospel." There are the interests and attractions of the present world, which, since the love of them is necessarily disturbed by the announcement that the world to come offers what is much more to be desired, operate, sometimes it may be in a manner which is not suspected, in hardening the heart against listening to and receiving that gospel. I think that in this way only can it be accounted for that the passages of Scripture which unequivocally declare the salvation of all men are comparatively unattended to, whilst belief is generally expressed in those supposed to be of opposite import. I am apprehensive that on the same accounts the arguments by which I have endeavoured to show that the latter passages admit of being interpreted consistently with the others, will receive little attention.

There exists, moreover, in the present day so long-standing and so general an inability to discern the inner and true sense of Scripture, "the letter which killeth" having been preferred to "the spirit which maketh alive," that it has become a matter of much difficulty to comprehend and explain the terms in which the gospel in its entirety is therein proclaimed, and either to give, or to receive, instruction which may conduce to an intelligent acceptance of it. In addition to which there prevails a tendency to rely on traditional and formal doctrine, and to assign to it an authority co-ordinate with that of Scripture, although as having had its origin at times when primitive faith and knowledge had in great measure declined, and "the mystery of iniquity" was already working, it cannot but be mixed with a human element of untruth. This tendency, which appears to be attributable to a consciousness of inability to form an independent judgment of the truths of Scripture, operates at present in creating a prejudice against all attempts to go beyond the boundaries by which Scriptural knowledge is assumed to be circumscribed. Nevertheless, regarding it as a duty to employ the opportunities and the ability which God has given me in making such an attempt, I have endeavoured to place the doctrine of the salvation and immortality of all men on a Scriptural basis, and I have now only to ask for an unprejudiced consideration of the arguments I have adduced for that purpose.

I have allowed to stand in the Essay (pp. 76-81) the views I held at the time it was composed respecting the interpretation of Matt. xxv. 46, because I considered that these views, although in certain respects they are inconsistent with those I maintain in this Appendix, might contribute, by comparison with the latter, towards an understanding of the passage. The interpretation which, after long consideration, I have finally adopted, was first published in two letters, contained under the head of "Correspondence," in the numbers of the *Guardian* for December 27, 1877, and January 16, 1878. With the view of offering some additional arguments in support of that interpretation, and making it more generally intelligible, I propose to begin with producing *in extenso* the two letters referred to.

"ETERNAL PUNISHMENT.

"Sir,

"After reading attentively the letters of your correspondents to which the sermon of Dr. Farrar has given occasion, it appeared to me that some views in addition to those which have hitherto been proposed, and in certain respects controverting them, may be worthy of consideration. I beg, therefore, to be allowed space for making the following remarks:—

"We are taught in the Scriptures that hereafter there will be a new constitution of the universe, 'new heavens and a new earth wherein dwelleth righteousness' (2 Peter iii. 13), and that in this perfect social state 'there shall be no more death, neither sorrow, nor crying, neither shall there be any more pain' (Rev. xxi. 4). To reconcile this revelation, so intelligible and so comprehensive, with the meaning of passages which seem to say that the punishment of the wicked will be 'endless,' presents a very great difficulty. We are not at liberty in such cases to accept some parts of Scripture and reject others in order to get rid of the difficulty, but must believe that the truth, if it should be reached, will establish the consistency of all, and that seeming contradictions are only due to our ignorance. I propose for consideration the following solution of the above-stated difficulty:—

"Jesus Christ in his ministration on earth said, in the course of giving instruction to his *disciples* (Matt. xxiv. 3), 'These [on the left hand] shall go into eternal punishment, and the righteous into eternal life' (Matt. xxv. 46). Considering that in all he said and did he had in view his Father's purpose of making the spirits of men meet for immortality, it may be asked, In what way was such teaching contributory to this end? May we not conclude from our Lord's words, apart from all other inferences, that eternal life is necessarily preceded by righteousness, and eternal punishment is as necessarily consequent upon sin, and that the knowledge of these divine decrees contributes to the formation of spirits for the life to come? This inference might be accepted as abstractedly true; but then the question arises, What is meant by *duration* as signified by the word 'eternal'? It should be remarked that in the statement of the doctrine I have employed the word 'necessarily' in a sense that is not unusual, and is generally thought to be intelligible. But it is to be taken into account that no such use of the term occurs in Scripture, where, in fact, it would be wholly incongruous. The reason of this is that the Scriptures contain no abstract truths which are not expressed, or expressible, in terms understood from the facts and conditions of human experience. This may especially be said of the discourses of our Lord, in consequence of which they are much misunderstood by the many who are incapable of discerning the spiritual through the literal, who, as he said, 'have eyes and see not, and ears and hear not.' Assuming, therefore, that there is truth in speaking of righteousness and life as being *necessarily* connected, as also of sin and punishment as being in like manner connected, we have to inquire in what way these abstract truths are expressed in the language of Scripture. I venture to make answer that this is done by its recognition of a special faculty we are all conscious of possessing, that of thinking and speaking of time (and space also) as indefinitely extended. (The mathematician knows that without the supposition, whether as to greatness or smallness, of *ad libitum* extent of space and time, he is unable to conduct his reasoning.) On this principle Scripture speaks of duration through 'ages, and ages,' because by such emphatic reference to our capacity for thinking of unlimited duration, the anterior necessity of certain abstract truths, as especially the being and attributes of Deity, and the characters of divine judgment, is expressed in terms drawn from common thought and experience.

"But the omnipotent Creator, who, for purposes towards us, made time and space to be what we perceive them to be, has also the power to change or *unmake* them. If it were not so, there would be a power above that of the Creator, which is impossible. The difficulty concerning the duration of future punishment appears to be attributable to a preconception tacitly, perhaps unconsciously, entertained by most persons that time and space have an independent existence, although the teaching of Scripture is directly opposed to this view. St. Paul speaks of 'height' and 'depth' as of things *created* (Rom. viii. 39); St. Peter has, 'One day is with the Lord as a thousand years, and a thousand years as one day' (2 Epist. iii. 8); and in Rev. x. 6 it is expressly said that when the scheme of redemption is finished 'time shall be no more.' The foregoing argument suffices, I think, to show that 'endless'˙ and eternal are not convertible terms, for the special reason that the latter is significant of time as being derived from *Œtas*, whereas the other has *per se* no necessary relation to time. (For the same etymological reason I consider 'eternal' to be preferable to 'ever-lasting.') I cannot forbear adverting here to a serious misstatement, as it seems to me, in Mr. Churton's letter in the Guardian of December 12 (p. 1714). He says that the teaching of Holy Scripture as to the matter of *duration*, is precisely the same with respect to eternal life and eternal death, having apparently overlooked the remarkable expression in Heb. vii. 16, 'indissoluble life' (*zôês akatalytou*), in which endlessness is signified by an epithet not explicitly indicative of time. No such epithet is applied in Scripture to future punishment. This difference is of great importance when taken with reference to the declaration in Scripture that time itself has an end.

"It would certainly appear that the apostle Paul did not teach that the future punishment of the wicked will be endless; otherwise, how could he have written, 'God is the Saviour of all men, specially of those that believe' (I Tim. iv. 10)? Is not this to assert that all are saved in the same sense that some who believe are saved, although there may be difference as to the order or mode of the salvation? We know that in the present age faith avails to save if it rests on the assurance given by the suffering and death of Jesus Christ that by passing through the same gate of suffering we are prepared to enter into life; for such faith yields the fruit of patience and righteousness. But *in the age to come* there is neither faith, nor repentance, nor *probation*, but 'a certain fearful looking for of judgment and fiery indignation' (Heb. x. 27). The appointed Judge is the Son of man, who, having suffered an unjust and painful death at the hands of sinful men, is entitled to execute the vengeance on sinners. All men are judged; but the elect, who have been sealed by faith and good works, escape condemnation, and are those that are 'specially' saved. The rest are condemned to undergo *the second death*. This is that 'threefold woe' and 'great tribulation' so plainly foretold in Scripture. It was by these 'terrors of the Lord' that St. Paul sought to 'persuade' men, and not, as it would seem, by saying that the misery will be without end. As matter of experience, the preaching of this hopeless destiny does not deter from sin, but only makes sad tender spirits whom God has not made sad. Why should we not rather believe that the purpose of avenging justice is fulfilled when that great and final tribulation (Mark xiii. 19) has availed, in virtue of the suffering whereby the Son of God 'consecrated' the way to life, for the *purification* and salvation of the condemned, seeing that even saints and martyrs have need to be purified by suffering (see Dan. xii. 10)? This view reconciles all apparent contradictions, and accords with the gospel declared in Rev. xxi. In making the foregoing statements I have necessarily tried to be brief; but I hope, ere long, to be able to publish a justification of them by arguments drawn at greater length from Scripture.

"Cambridge, December 21, 1877."

"ETERNAL LIFE.

"After the publication of my letter in the *Guardian* of December 27 (p. 1786), I received from various quarters interrogations and arguments, which led me to see that there was an omission in one part of my reasoning, by supplying which the whole of the argument might be made much more complete. In particular, it was maintained by my correspondents, I admit quite logically, that if eternal punishment in Matt. xxv. 4:6 could be taken to mean punishment which has an end, by parity of reasoning 'eternal life' must there mean life which has an end. As I find that the same argument has been adduced in the correspondence of the *Guardian*, I hope I may be allowed, notwithstanding the length to which the discussion of the subject has gone, the opportunity of a supplementary letter for showing how, by rectifying the above-mentioned defect, the views I have proposed meet this difficulty.

"In the Scriptures definite mention is made of only two ages, the present age and the future age, or, in other words, 'this world and the world to come' (Matt. xii. 32). The plural ages (*aiônes*) and 'ages of ages' are expressions to which we can by no mental effort attach a definite signification, and consequently, as I endeavoured to show in my former letter, they admit of various abstract applications. As in the present age, so in the age to come, there is a *succession* of events which take place under conditions of time. These events have received comparatively but small attention in the theology of the present day, apparently because it is not generally seen that they are spoken of much more largely by the prophets of the Old Testament than in the New Testament, in which it is assumed that the old prophets are understood; and again, because the epitome given in the Book of Revelation (see Rev. x. 7) of the communications vouchsafed to the prophets is expressed in symbols which we find it hard to interpret. There are, however, passages in the New Testament which expressly make known the relation of deeds and events of the present age to those of the age to come; as especially our Lord's discourse 'as he sat on the Mount of Olives,' and the apostles 'Peter and James and John and Andrew' asked Him privately to tell them what would be the sign of his coming, and of *the end of the world* (*tês synteleias tou aiônos*). There is also that remarkable passage in which St. Matthew records that Jesus said to Peter, 'Ye who have followed me, in the regeneration when the Son of man shall sit on the throne of his glory, ye also shall sit on twelve thrones, judging the twelve tribes of Israel.' The number 'twelve' in Scripture symbolism always signifies 'election;' the judges may be presumed to be of the order of prophets and apostles—the elect of the elect—and the twelve tribes of Israel the whole number of the elect (see Rev. vii. 4-8). Now, these twelve times twelve thousand, symbolizing the complete number of the redeemed of every age and nation, are 'the firstfruits unto God and to the Lamb,' and being made perfect by suffering and judgment, farther on in the events of that age 'follow the Lamb whithersoever he goeth,' and together with him execute the final judgment on the whole world (Rev. xix. 14), inclusive even of the judgment on Satan and his angels. This doctrine seems to have been generally taught in the days of the apostles, inasmuch as St. Paul writes to the Corinthians (I Epist. vi. 2, 3), 'Know ye not that the saints shall judge the world?' 'Know ye not that we shall judge angels?' Even in the Psalms we read, 'This honour have all His saints' (see Psalm cxlix. 6-9).

"On these premises, it seems to me, the following argument may be founded relative to the interpretation of Matt. xxv. 46. In that chapter the *separation* between the sheep and the goats is spoken of as initiatory to the general judgment, and the chapter closes with an exposition of the principles on which the judgment is conducted as regards both the one class and the other. The details and the processes of the judgment, together with its *results*, are to be sought for in the writings of the prophets and in the Book of Revelation. Now, when account is taken of all events of that future life, it may be said, I think, with truth, that the righteous who live and act in it throughout, when that life begins enter into 'eternal life,' the word 'eternal' being applicable because that age has a time-limit. *This* eternal life, the mention of which was omitted in the former letter, merges into endless, or indissoluble, life, when time is no more, and words expressive of time cease to have application. In an analogous manner the unrighteous may be said to go into 'eternal punishment' when they enter upon the experience of the future age, the limit of the effects of the judgment and punishment which they are doomed to undergo being a 'second death.' However great and terrible may be the woe and tribulation attendant on that event, we know as matter of experience of life at present, that death, of itself, is but a passage into another state of existence. We have, therefore, no right to affirm that after the effects of judgment and punishment are accomplished, the second death is not a transition into that state of things in the new heavens and new earth which is described in Rev. xxi. Rather, may we not conclude that eternal life and eternal punishment terminate alike with the end of time, and that in the consummation of all things both are merged in indissoluble life, that God may be all in all? This conclusion appears to meet the difficulty stated at the beginning of this letter.

"I take this opportunity for expressing my approval of the arrangement of the New Lectionary, by which chapters of the Book of Revelation are now read more frequently than formerly before the people, this portion of Scripture being indispensable for communicating to them the doctrine of Jesus Christ in all its integrity.

"Cambridge, January 12, 1878."

The difficulty experienced in the present day of rightly apprehending the doctrine taught by our Lord in Matt. xxv. 46, and in like passages, arises, according to the arguments contained in the Essay and in the foregoing letters, from the little attention that is paid in the Christian doctrine now generally accepted to what the Scriptures reveal respecting "the age to come" (*aiôn ho mellôn*) as distinguished from "the present age" (*aiôn outos, aiôn ho parôn*). The designation "age" applied in common to both, indicates that each has a beginning and an ending. The future age begins at the termination of the present age, the separation between them being the epoch of a resurrection of the dead—not, however, of all the dead, but "a resurrection of the just," that is, of those who have been prepared and sealed by faith, and suffering, and good works, in the present life, for immediate entrance into a new state of life. It is said of these that "they cannot die any more, and are the children of God, being the children of the resurrection" (Luke xx. 36). These are they who "have part in the first resurrection," of whom it is further said that "they *lived* and reigned with Christ a thousand years," whereas of "the rest of the dead" it is said that "they *lived* not till the thousand years were finished" (see Rev. xx. 4, 6). It is plain, therefore, that there will be a time of *separation* of the one class from the other—the time of *threshing*, when the tares are separated from the wheat; and that whilst the elect at that time enter into the Œonian life (that is, the life of the age to come), the rest of the dead when they live again enter into a state in which they undergo "Œonian punishment" (that is, punishment that pertains to the age to come), ending eventually in the second death, which, however, in common with all divine punishment, is inflicted for producing a certain effect foreordained in the counsels of the Almighty. (Respecting this effect, see what I have said in the Essay and at the end of the first of the foregoing letters.)

That the words of the passage in St. Matthew might be understood, at least by the disciples to whom they were addressed, in the sense above indicated, may be inferred from the knowledge of the religious Jews of that time respecting the events of the future age, as conveyed to them by the writings of the prophets of the Old Testament, with which they were familiar. In proof of the general diffusion of such knowledge we may cite the response of Martha to the Lord respecting the resurrection of Lazarus, "I know that he shall rise again at the resurrection in the last day" (John xi. 24), and the common belief of a resurrection of the dead entertained by the numerous sect of the Pharisees, as well as the particular character of the unbelief of the smaller body of Sadducees (see Acts xxiii. 8, where it is stated that "the Sadducees say that there is no resurrection, neither angel, nor spirit: but the Pharisees confess both"). It is hard to perceive etymologically how the word *aiôuios* could have received the meaning "ever-*lasting*." There is, in fact, a very remarkable passage of the Apocalypse in which that meaning is quite excluded: "And I saw another angel fly in the midst of heaven, having the gospel of the age to come to preach (*euaggelion aiônion euaggelisai*) unto them that dwell on the earth, and to every nation, and kindred, and tongue, and people, saying with a loud voice, Fear God, and give glory to Him; for the hour of His judgment is come: and worship Him that made heaven, and earth, and the sea, and the fountains of waters" (Rev. xiv. 6, 7). It is evident that if *aiônion euaggelion* here meant an everlasting gospel, the event which the good news is intended to announce would never come. It may, perhaps, be asserted that this passage of the Apocalypse refers to a gospel announcement taking place at the present time, considering that a distinctive feature of this age is a large increase of the knowledge of the facts and laws of nature, and that possibly, contemporaneously with such knowledge, God may vouchsafe a fuller understanding of the Book of Revelation, and a discernment of the Œonian gospel it proclaims (compare Dan. xii. 3, 4). That the true interpretation of the Apocalypse will eventually be reached is implied by the words, "Seal not the sayings of the prophecy of this book" (Rev. xxii. 10).

On reconsidering the arguments of the Essay it occurred to me that it would be proper to take notice in the Appendix of one other subject. In pages 9, 15, and 63 the doctrine that immortality is dependent on a state of perfected righteousness is regarded as "self-evident." I now think that the use of that term is objectionable, inasmuch as, according to the title of the Essay, every such statement ought to rest wholly on Scriptural ground. I propose, therefore, to adduce here passages of Scripture which indicate an intimate relation between righteousness and life. Out of many texts which might be cited for this purpose, I have selected two, as follows. First, when under the law, Moses said to the Israelites, "I have set before you life and death: choose life," they must have understood his words as signifying that on condition of submission to the will of God and obedience to His righteous laws, they might look forward in faith to the enjoyment of the future covenanted life. (See what is said on this text in p. 28.) Again, the same dependence of life on righteousness forms an essential part of the Gospel of Jesus Christ, although taught in a different manner. St. Paul, for instance, has given in Rom. v. 18, the following summary of Christian doctrine. Therefore as through one transgression (__di henos paraptômatos_), unto all men, unto condemnation (*eis katakrima*), so through one righteousness (*di henos dikaiômatos*, i.e. the obedience unto death of Jesus Christ), unto all men, unto life-justification (*eis dikaiôsin zôês*), where, it should be noticed, *zôês* is not a dependent genitive, but, as in many instances in New Testament Greek, a genitive of quality. Thus this text declares that the justification of all men, which is their being eventually made righteous through the operation of the Son of God, has the quality of conferring *life*.